D0753735

# Canvas
*Pocket Reference*

# Canvas
*Pocket Reference*

*David Flanagan*

Beijing · Cambridge · Farnham · Köln · Sebastopol · Tokyo

**Canvas Pocket Reference**
by David Flanagan

Published by O'Reilly Media, Inc., 1005 Gravenstein Highway North, Sebastopol, CA 95472.

O'Reilly books may be purchased for educational, business, or sales promotional use. Online editions are also available for most titles (*http://my.safari booksonline.com*). For more information, contact our corporate/institutional sales department: (800) 998-9938 or *corporate@oreilly.com*.

**Editors:**   Mike Loukides and Simon St. Laurent
**Production Editor:**   Teresa Elsey
**Proofreader:**   Sada Preisch
**Indexer:**   John Bickelhaupt
**Cover Designer:**   Karen Montgomery
**Interior Designer:**   David Futato
**Illustrator:**   Robert Romano

**Printing History:**
December 2010:          First Edition.

ISBN: 978-1-449-39680-0

[TM]

1291303034

# Contents

# Preface

This book documents the JavaScript API for drawing graphics in an HTML `<canvas>` tag. It assumes that you know the JavaScript programming language and have at least basic familiarity with the use of JavaScript in web pages. Chapter 1 is a tutorial that explains all Canvas features and demonstrates them with examples. Chapter 2 is a reference to each of the Canvas-related classes, methods, and properties.

This book is an excerpt from the much longer book *JavaScript: The Definitive Guide*; my publisher and I felt that the `<canvas>` tag is such an exciting feature of HTML5 that it deserves a timely and concise book of its own. Because the Canvas API is relatively small, this short book can document it definitively.

Thanks to Raffaele Cecco for a careful review of the book and its code examples. Thanks also to my editor, Mike Loukides, for his enthusiasm for this project and to editor Simon St. Laurent for his work converting the material from "Definitive Guide" to "Pocket Reference" format.

The examples in this book can be downloaded from the book's web page, which will also include errata if any errors are discovered after publication:

*http://oreilly.com/catalog/0636920016045/*

In general, you may use the examples in this book in your programs and documentation. You do not need to contact us for permission unless you're reproducing a significant portion of the code. We appreciate, but do not require, an attribution like this: "From *Canvas Pocket Reference* by David Flanagan (O'Reilly). Copyright 2011 David Flanagan, 978-1-449-39680-0." If you feel your use of code examples falls outside fair use or the permission given here, feel free to contact us at *permissions@oreilly.com*.

To comment or ask technical questions about this book, send email to:

*bookquestions@oreilly.com*

This book is also available from the Safari Books Online service. For full digital access to this book and others on similar topics from O'Reilly and other publishers, sign up at *http://my.safaribooksonline.com*.

# CHAPTER 1

# Canvas Tutorial

This book explains how to draw graphics in web pages using JavaScript and the HTML `<canvas>` tag. The ability to dynamically generate sophisticated graphics in the web browser instead of downloading them from a server is revolutionary:

- The code used to produce graphics on the client side is typically much smaller than the images themselves, creating a substantial bandwidth savings.

- Offloading drawing tasks from the server to the client reduces the load on the server, potentially saving on hardware costs.

- Generating graphics on the client is consistent with the Ajax application architecture in which servers provide data and clients manage the presentation of that data.

- The client can rapidly and dynamically redraw graphics, enabling graphically intense applications (such as games and simulations) that are simply not feasible when each frame has to be downloaded from a server.

- Writing graphics programs is fun, and the `<canvas>` tag gives web developers some relief from the drudgery of the DOM!

The `<canvas>` tag has no appearance of its own but creates a drawing surface within the document and exposes a powerful drawing API to client-side JavaScript. The `<canvas>` tag is standardized by HTML5 but has been around for longer than that. It was introduced by Apple in Safari 1.3, and has been supported by Firefox since version 1.5 and Opera since version 9. It is also supported in all versions of Chrome. The `<canvas>` tag is not supported by IE before IE 9, but can be reasonably well emulated in IE 6, 7, and 8.

---

## Using the Canvas in IE

To use the `<canvas>` tag in IE 6, 7, or 8, download the open-source ExplorerCanvas project from *http://code.google.com/p/ explorercanvas/*. After unpacking the project, include the "excanvas" script in the `<head>` of your web pages using an Internet Explorer conditional comment like this:

```
<!--[if lte IE 8]>
<script src="excanvas.compiled.js"></script>
<![endif]-->
```

With those lines at the top of your web pages, `<canvas>` tags and basic Canvas drawing commands will work in IE. Radial gradients and clipping are not supported. Line width does not scale correctly when the X and Y dimensions are scaled by different amounts, and you can expect to see other minor rendering differences in IE as well.

---

Most of the Canvas drawing API is defined not on the `<canvas>` element itself but instead on a "drawing context" object obtained with the `getContext()` method of the canvas. Call `getContext()` with the argument "2d" to obtain a CanvasRenderingContext2D object that you can use to draw two-dimensional graphics into the canvas. It is important to understand that the canvas element and its context object are two very different objects. Because it has such a long class name, I do not often refer to the CanvasRenderingContext2D object by name and instead simply call it the "context object." Similarly, when I write about the "Canvas API" I usually mean "the methods of the CanvasRenderingContext2D object." Also, since the long class name CanvasRenderingContext2D does not fit well on these narrow pages, the reference section that follows this tutorial chapter abbreviates it as CRC.

---

### 3D Graphics in a Canvas

At the time of this writing, browser vendors are starting to implement a 3D graphics API for the <canvas> tag. The API is known as WebGL, and is a JavaScript binding to the OpenGL standard API. To obtain a context object for 3D graphics, pass the string "webgl" to the getContext() method of the canvas. WebGL is a large, complicated, and low-level API that is not documented in this book: web developers are more likely to use utility libraries built on top of WebGL than to use the WebGL API directly.

---

As a simple example of the Canvas API, the following code draws a red square and blue circle into <canvas> tags to produce output like that shown in Figure 1-1:

```
<body>
This is a red square:
<canvas id="square" width=10 height=10></canvas>.
This is a blue circle:
<canvas id="circle" width=10 height=10></canvas>.
<script>
// Get first canvas element and its context
var canvas = document.getElementById("square");
var context = canvas.getContext("2d");
// Draw something in the canvas
context.fillStyle = "#f00";  // Set color to red
context.fillRect(0,0,10,10); // Fill a small square

// Get second canvas and its context
canvas = document.getElementById("circle");
context = canvas.getContext("2d");
// Begin a path and add a circle to it
context.beginPath();
context.arc(5, 5, 5, 0, 2*Math.PI, true);
context.fillStyle = "#00f";  // Set blue fill
context.fill();              // Fill the path
</script>
</body>
```

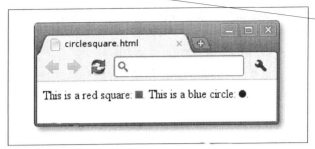

*Figure 1-1. Simple canvas graphics*

The Canvas API describes complex shapes as a "path" of lines and curves that can be drawn or filled. A path is defined by a series of method calls, such as the beginPath() and arc() invocations in the preceding code. Once a path is defined, other methods, such as fill(), operate on that path. Various properties of the context object, such as fillStyle, specify how these operations are performed. The subsections that follow explain:

- How to define paths, how to draw or "stroke" the outline of a path, and how to fill the interior of a path
- How to set and query the graphics attributes of the canvas context object, and how to save and restore the current state of those attributes
- Canvas dimensions, the default canvas coordinate system, and how to transform that coordinate system
- The various curve-drawing methods defined by the Canvas API
- Some special-purpose utility methods for drawing rectangles
- How to specify colors, work with transparency, and draw with color gradients and repeating image patterns
- The attributes that control line width and the appearance of line endpoints and vertices
- How to draw text in a <canvas>

---

- How to "clip" graphics so that no drawing is done outside of a region you specify
- How to add drop shadows to your graphics
- How to draw (and optionally scale) images into a canvas, and how to extract the contents of a canvas as an image
- How to control the compositing process by which newly drawn (translucent) pixels are combined with the existing pixels in the canvas
- How to query and set the raw red, green, blue, and alpha (transparency) values of the pixels in the canvas
- How to determine whether a mouse event occurred above something you've drawn in a canvas

This chapter ends with a practical example that uses <canvas> tags to render small inline charts known as *spark-lines*. This tutorial chapter is followed by a reference section that documents the Canvas API in complete detail.

Much of the <canvas> example code that follows operates on a variable called c. This variable holds the CanvasRenderingContext2D object of the canvas, but the code to initialize that variable it is not typically shown. In order to make these examples run, you would need to add HTML markup to define a canvas with appropriate width and height attributes, and then add code like this to initialize the variable c:

```
var canvas = document.getElementById("my_canvas_id");
var c = canvas.getContext('2d');
```

The figures that follow were all generated by JavaScript code drawing into a <canvas> tag—typically into a large offscreen canvas to produce high-resolution print-quality graphics.

# Drawing Lines and Filling Polygons

To draw lines on a canvas and to fill the areas enclosed by those lines, you begin by defining a *path*. A path is a sequence of one or more subpaths. A subpath is a sequence of two or more points connected by line segments (or, as we'll see later, by curve segments). Begin a new path with the beginPath() method. Begin a new subpath with the moveTo() method. Once you have established the starting point of a subpath with moveTo(), you can connect that point to a new point with a straight line by calling lineTo(). The following code defines a path that includes two line segments:

```
c.beginPath();      // Start a new path
c.moveTo(20, 20);   // Begin a subpath at (20,20)
c.lineTo(120, 120); // Add a line to (120,120)
c.lineTo(20, 120);  // Another from there to (20,120)
```

The preceding code simply defines a path; it does not draw anything on the canvas. To draw (or "stroke") the two line segments in the path, call the stroke() method, and to fill the area defined by those line segments, call fill():

```
c.fill();    // Fill a triangular area
c.stroke();  // Stroke two sides of the triangle
```

The preceding code (along with some additional code to set line widths and fill colors) produced the drawing shown in Figure 1-2.

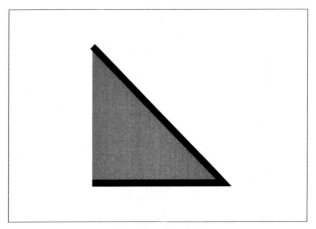

*Figure 1-2. A simple path, filled and stroked*

Notice that the subpath defined previously is "open." It consists of just two line segments, and the endpoint is not connected back to the starting point. This means that it does not enclose a region. The fill() method fills open subpaths by acting as if a straight line connected the last point in the subpath to the first point in the subpath. That is why the preceding code fills a triangle, but strokes only two sides of the triangle.

If you wanted to stroke all three sides of the triangle shown previously, you would call the closePath() method to connect the endpoint of the subpath to the start point. (You could also call lineTo(20,20), but then you end up with three line segments that share a start and endpoint but are not truly closed. When drawing with wide lines, the visual results are better if you use closePath().)

There are two other important points to notice about stroke() and fill(). First, both methods operate on all subpaths in the current path. Suppose we had added another subpath in the code:

```
c.moveTo(300,100); // Begin a new subpath at (300,100)
c.lineTo(300,200); // Draw a vertical line to (300,200)
```

Then when we called stroke() we would have drawn two connected edges of a triangle and a disconnected vertical line.

The second point to note about stroke() and fill() is that neither one alters the current path: you can call fill() and the path will still be there when you call stroke(). When you are done with a path and want to begin another you must remember to call beginPath(). If you don't you'll end up adding new subpaths to the existing path and you may end up drawing those old subpaths over and over again.

Example 1-1 defines a function for drawing regular polygons and demonstrates the use of moveTo(), lineTo(), and closePath() for defining subpaths and of fill() and stroke() for drawing those paths. It produces the drawing shown in Figure 1-3.

*Example 1-1. Regular polygons with moveTo(), lineTo(), and closePath()*

```
// Define a regular polygon with n sides, centered at (x,y)
// with radius r. The vertices are equally spaced along the
// circumference of a circle. Put the first vertex straight
// up or at the specified angle. Rotate clockwise, unless
// the last argument is true.
function polygon(c,n,x,y,r,angle,counterclockwise) {
    angle = angle || 0;
    counterclockwise = counterclockwise || false;
    // Compute vertex position and begin a subpath there
    c.moveTo(x + r*Math.sin(angle),
             y - r*Math.cos(angle));
    var delta = 2*Math.PI/n;    // Angle between vertices
    for(var i = 1; i < n; i++) { // For remaining vertices
        // Compute angle of this vertex
        angle += counterclockwise?-delta:delta;
        // Compute position of vertex and add a line to it
        c.lineTo(x + r*Math.sin(angle),
                 y - r*Math.cos(angle));
    }
    c.closePath(); // Connect last vertex back to the first
}

// Start a new path and add polygon subpaths
c.beginPath();
polygon(c, 3, 50, 70, 50);              // Triangle
polygon(c, 4, 150, 60, 50, Math.PI/4);  // Square
polygon(c, 5, 255, 55, 50);             // Pentagon
polygon(c, 6, 365, 53, 50, Math.PI/6);  // Hexagon
// Add a small counterclockwise square inside the hexagon
polygon(c, 4, 365, 53, 20, Math.PI/4, true);

// Set properties that control how the graphics will look
c.fillStyle = "#ccc";     // Light-gray interiors
c.strokeStyle = "#008";   // outlined with dark-blue lines
c.lineWidth = 5;          // five pixels wide.

// Now draw all the polygons (each in its own subpath)
c.fill();                 // Fill the shapes
c.stroke();               // And stroke their outlines
```

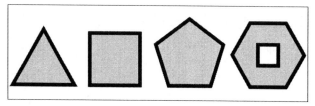

*Figure 1-3. Regular polygons*

Notice that this example draws a hexagon with a square inside it. The square and the hexagon are separate subpaths but they overlap. When this happens (or when a single subpath intersects itself) the canvas needs to be able to determine which regions are inside the path and which are outside. The canvas uses a test known as the "nonzero winding rule" to achieve this. In this case, the interior of the square is not filled because the square and the hexagon were drawn in opposite directions: the vertices of the hexagon were connected with line segments moving clockwise around the circle. The vertices of the square were connected counterclockwise. Had the square been drawn clockwise as well, the call to `fill()` would have filled the interior of the square.

---

## The Nonzero Winding Rule

To test whether a point P is inside a path, using the nonzero winding rule, imagine a ray drawn from P, in any direction, off to infinity (or, more practically, to some point outside of the path's bounding box). Now initialize a counter to zero and enumerate all places where the path crosses the ray. Each time the path crosses the ray in a clockwise direction, add one to the count. Each time the path crosses the ray counterclockwise, subtract one from the count. If, after all crossings have been enumerated, the count is nonzero, then the point P is inside the path. If, on the other hand, the count is zero, then P is outside the path.

---

# Graphics Attributes

Example 1-1 set the properties `fillStyle`, `strokeStyle`, and `lineWidth` on the context object of the canvas. These properties are graphics attributes that specify the color to be used by `fill()`, the color to be used by `stroke()`, and the width of the lines to be drawn by `stroke()`. Notice that these parameters are not passed to the `fill()` and `stroke()` methods, but are instead part of the general *graphics state* of the canvas. If you define a method that draws a shape and do not set these properties yourself, then the caller of your method can define the color of the shape by setting the `strokeStyle` and `fillStyle` properties before calling your method. This separation of graphics state from drawing commands is fundamental to the Canvas API and is akin to the separation of presentation from content achieved by applying cascading stylesheets (CSS) to HTML documents.

The Canvas API defines 15 graphics attribute properties on the CanvasRenderingContext2D object. These properties are listed in Table 1-1 and explained in detail in the relevant sections following.

*Table 1-1. Graphics attributes of the Canvas API*

| Property | Meaning |
| --- | --- |
| fillStyle | The color, gradient, or pattern for fills |
| font | The CSS font for text-drawing commands |
| globalAlpha | Transparency to be added to all pixels drawn |
| globalCompositeOperation | How to combine pixel colors |
| lineCap | How the ends of lines are rendered |
| lineJoin | How vertices are rendered |
| lineWidth | The width of stroked lines |
| miterLimit | Maximum length of acute mitered vertices |
| textAlign | Horizontal alignment of text |
| textBaseline | Vertical alignment of text |

| Property | Meaning |
|---|---|
| shadowBlur | How crisp or fuzzy shadows are |
| shadowColor | The color of drop shadows |
| shadowOffsetX | The horizontal offset of shadows |
| shadowOffsetY | The vertical offset of shadows |
| strokeStyle | The color, gradient, or pattern for lines |

Since the Canvas API defines graphics attributes on the context object, you might be tempted to call `getContext()` multiple times to obtain multiple context objects. If you could do this, then you could define different attributes on each context: each context would then be like a different brush and would paint with a different color, or draw lines of different widths. Unfortunately, you cannot use the canvas in this way. Each <canvas> tag has only a single context object, and every call to `getContext()` returns the same CanvasRenderingContext2D object.

Although the Canvas API only allows you to define a single set of graphics attributes at a time, it does allow you to save the current graphics state so that you can alter it and then easily restore it later. The `save()` method pushes the current graphics state onto a stack of saved states. The `restore()` method pops the stack and restores the most recently saved state. All of the properties listed in Table 1-1 are part of the saved state, as are the current transformation and clipping region (both are explained later). Importantly, the currently defined path and the current point are not part of the graphics state and cannot be saved and restored.

If you need more flexibility than a simple stack of graphics states allows, you may find it helpful to define utility methods like the ones shown in Example 1-2.

*Example 1-2. Graphics state management utilities*

```
// Revert to the last saved graphics state,
// without popping the stack of saved states.
CanvasRenderingContext2D.prototype.revert = function() {
```

```
    this.restore(); // Restore the old graphics state
    this.save();    // Save it again so we can go back to it
    return this;    // Allow method chaining
};

// Set the graphics attributes specified by the properties
// of the object o. Or, if no argument is passed, return
// the current attributes as an object. Note that this does
// not handle the transformation or clipping region.
CanvasRenderingContext2D.prototype.attrs = function(o) {
    if (o) {
        for(var a in o)       // For each property in o
            this[a] = o[a];   // Set it as an attribute
        return this;          // Enable method chaining
    }
    else return {
        fillStyle: this.fillStyle,
        font: this.font,
        globalAlpha: this.globalAlpha,
        globalCompositeOperation:
            this.globalCompositeOperation,
        lineCap: this.lineCap,
        lineJoin: this.lineJoin,
        lineWidth: this.lineWidth,
        miterLimit: this.miterLimit,
        textAlign: this.textAlign,
        textBaseline: this.textBaseline,
        shadowBlur: this.shadowBlur,
        shadowColor: this.shadowColor,
        shadowOffsetX: this.shadowOffsetX,
        shadowOffsetY: this.shadowOffsetY,
        strokeStyle: this.strokeStyle
    };
};
```

# Canvas Dimensions and Coordinates

The width and height attributes of the <canvas> tag and the
corresponding width and height properties of the Canvas object specify the dimensions of the canvas. The default canvas
coordinate system places the origin (0,0) at the upper-left corner of the canvas. X coordinates increase to the right and Y
coordinates increase as you go down the screen. Points on the

canvas can be specified using floating-point values, and these are not automatically rounded to integers—the canvas uses anti-aliasing techniques to simulate partially filled pixels.

The dimensions of a canvas are so fundamental that they cannot be altered without completely resetting the canvas. Setting either the `width` or `height` properties of a canvas (even setting them to their current value) clears the canvas, erases the current path, and resets all graphics attributes (including current transformation and clipping region) to their original state.

Despite this fundamental importance, canvas dimensions do not necessarily match either the onscreen size of the canvas or the number of pixels that make up the canvas drawing surface. Canvas dimensions (and also the default coordinate system) are measured in CSS pixels. CSS pixels are usually the same thing as regular pixels. On high-resolution displays, however, implementations are allowed to map multiple device pixels to single CSS pixels. This means that the rectangle of pixels that the canvas draws into may be larger than the canvas's nominal dimensions. You need to be aware of this when working with the pixel-manipulation features (see "Pixel Manipulation" on page 43) of the canvas, but the distinction between virtual CSS pixels and actual hardware pixels does not otherwise have any effect on the canvas code you write.

By default a `<canvas>` tag is displayed onscreen at the size (in CSS pixels) specified by its HTML `width` and `height` attributes. Like any HTML element, however, a `<canvas>` tag can have its onscreen size specified by CSS `width` and `height` style attributes. If you specify an onscreen size that is different than the actual dimensions of the canvas, then the pixels of the canvas are automatically scaled as needed to fit the screen dimensions specified by the CSS attributes. The onscreen size of the canvas does not affect the number of CSS or hardware pixels reserved in the canvas bitmap, and the scaling that is done is an image scaling operation. If the onscreen dimensions are substantially larger than the actual dimensions of the canvas, this results in pixelated graphics. This is an issue for graphic designers and does not affect canvas programming.

# Coordinate System Transforms

As noted above, the default coordinate system of a canvas places the origin in the upper-left corner, has X coordinates increasing to the right, and has Y coordinates increasing downward. In this default system, the coordinates of a point map directly to a CSS pixel (which then maps directly to one or more device pixels). Certain canvas operations and attributes (such as extracting raw pixel values and setting shadow offsets) always use this default coordinate system. In addition to the default coordinate system, however, every canvas has a "current transformation matrix" as part of its graphics state. This matrix defines the current coordinate system of the canvas. In most canvas operations, when you specify the coordinates of a point, it is taken to be a point in the current coordinate system, not in the default coordinate system. The current transformation matrix is used to convert the coordinates you specified to the equivalent coordinates in the default coordinate system.

The `setTransform()` method allows you to set a canvas's transformation matrix directly, but coordinate system transformations are usually easier to specify as a sequence of translations, rotations and scaling operations. Figure 1-4 illustrates these operations and their effect on the canvas coordinate system. The program that produced the figure drew the same set of axes seven times in a row. The only thing that changed each time was the current transform. Notice that the transforms affect the text as well as the lines that are drawn.

The `translate()` method simply moves the origin of the coordinate system left, right, up, or down. The `rotate()` method rotates the axes clockwise by the specified angle. (The Canvas API always specifies angles in radians. To convert degrees to radians, divide by 180 and multiply by `Math.PI`.) The `scale()` method stretches or contracts distances along the X or Y axes.

Passing a negative scale factor to the `scale()` method flips that axis across the origin, as if it were reflected in a mirror. This is what was done in the lower-left of Figure 1-4: `translate()` was

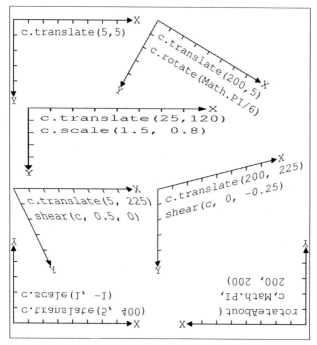

*Figure 1-4. Coordinate system transformations*

used to move the origin to the bottom-left corner of the canvas, and then scale() was used to flip the Y axis around so that Y coordinates increase as we go up the page. A flipped coordinate system like this is familiar from algebra class and may be useful for plotting data points on charts. Note, however, that it makes text difficult to read!

## Understanding Transformations Mathematically

I find it easiest to understand transforms geometrically and to think about translate(), rotate(), and scale() as transforming the axes of the coordinate system as illustrated in Figure 1-4. It is also possible to understand transforms algebraically as equations that map the coordinates of a point (x,y) in the transformed coordinate system back to the coordinates of the same point (x',y') in the previous coordinate system.

The method call `c.translate(dx,dy)` can be described with these equations:

```
// (0,0) in the new system is (dx,dy) in the old
x' = x + dx;
y' = y + dy;
```

Scaling operations have similarly simple equations. A call `c.scale(sx,sy)` can be described like this:

```
x' = sx * x;
y' = sy * y;
```

Rotations are more complicated. The call `c.rotate(a)` is described by these trigonometric equations:

```
x' = x * cos(a) - y * sin(a);
y' = y * cos(a) + x * sin(a);
```

Notice that the order of transformations matters. Suppose we start with the default coordinate system of a canvas, and then translate it and then scale it. In order to map the point (x,y) in the current coordinate system back to the point (x'',y'') in the default coordinate system, we must first apply the scaling equations to map the point to an intermediate point (x', y') in the translated but unscaled coordinate system, and then use the translation equations to map from this intermediate point to (x'',y''). The result is this:

```
x'' = sx*x + dx;
y'' = sy*y + dy;
```

If, on the other hand, we'd called `scale()` before calling `translate()`, the resulting equations would be different:

```
x'' = sx*(x + dx);
y'' = sy*(y + dy);
```

The key thing to remember when thinking algebraically about sequences of transformations is that you must work backward from the last (most recent) transformation to the first. When

---

thinking geometrically about transformed axes, however, you work forward from first transformation to last.

The transformations supported by the canvas are known as *affine transforms*. Affine transforms may modify the distances between points and the angles between lines, but parallel lines always remain parallel after an affine transformation—it is not possible, for example, to specify a fish-eye lens distortion with an affine transform. An arbitrary affine transform can be described by the six parameters a through f in these equations:

```
x' = ax + cy + e
y' = bx + dy + f
```

You can apply an arbitrary transformation to the current coordinate system by passing those six parameters to the `transform()` method. Figure 1-4 illustrates two types of transformations—shears and rotations about a specified point—that you can implement with the `transform()` method like this:

```
// Shear transform:
//   x' = x + kx*y;
//   y' = y + ky*x;
function shear(c, kx, ky) {
    c.transform(1, ky, kx, 1, 0, 0);
}

// Rotate theta radians clockwise around (x,y).
// This can also be accomplished with a translate,
// rotate, translate back sequence of transformations.
function rotateAbout(c, theta, x, y) {
    var ct = Math.cos(theta), st = Math.sin(theta);
    c.transform(ct, -st, st, ct,
                -x*ct-y*st+x, x*st-y*ct+y);
}
```

The `setTransform()` method takes the same arguments as `transform()`, but instead of transforming the current coordinate system, it ignores the current system, transforms the default coordinate system, and makes the result the new current coordinate system. `setTransform()` is useful to temporarily reset the canvas to its default coordinate system:

```
c.save();      // Save current coordinate system
// Revert to the default coordinate system
c.setTransform(1,0,0,1,0,0);
// Now draw using default CSS pixel coordinates
c.restore(); // Restore the saved coordinate system
```

## Transformation Example

Example 1-3 demonstrates the power of coordinate system transformations by using the `translate()`, `rotate()`, and `scale()` methods recursively to draw a Koch snowflake fractal. The output of this example appears in Figure 1-5, which shows Koch snowflakes with 0, 1, 2, 3, and 4 levels of recursion.

The code that produces these figures is elegant but its use of recursive coordinate system transformations makes it somewhat difficult to understand. Even if you don't follow all the nuances, note that the code includes only a single invocation of the `lineTo()` method. Every single line segment in Figure 1-5 is drawn like this:

```
c.lineTo(len, 0);
```

The value of the variable `len` does not change during the execution of the program, so the position, orientation, and length of each of the line segments is determined by translations, rotations, and scaling operations.

*Example 1-3. A Koch snowflake with transformations*

```
var deg = Math.PI/180;  // For converting degrees to radians

// Draw a level-n Koch Snowflake fractal in the context c,
// with lower-left corner at (x,y) and side length len.
function snowflake(c, n, x, y, len) {
    c.save();            // Save current transformation
    c.translate(x,y);    // Translate to starting point
    c.moveTo(0,0);       // Begin a new subpath there
    leg(n);              // Draw the first leg of the fractal
    c.rotate(-120*deg);  // Rotate 120 degrees anticlockwise
    leg(n);              // Draw the second leg
    c.rotate(-120*deg);  // Rotate again.
    leg(n);              // Draw the final leg
    c.closePath();       // Close the subpath
```

```
    c.restore();           // Restore original transformation

// Draw a single leg of a level-n Koch snowflake.
// This function leaves the current point at the end of
// the leg it has drawn and translates the coordinate
// system so the current point is (0,0). This means you
// can easily call rotate() after drawing a leg.
function leg(n) {
    c.save();              // Save current transform
    if (n == 0) {          // Non-recursive case:
        c.lineTo(len, 0);  //   Just a horizontal line
    }
    else { // Recursive case:
        //     draw 4 sub-legs like: ‾\/‾
        c.scale(1/3,1/3);  // Sub-legs are 1/3rd size
        leg(n-1);          // Draw the first sub-leg
        c.rotate(60*deg);  // Turn 60 degrees clockwise
        leg(n-1);          // Draw the second sub-leg
        c.rotate(-120*deg);// Rotate 120 degrees back
        leg(n-1);          // Third sub-leg
        c.rotate(60*deg);  // Back to original heading
        leg(n-1);          // Final sub-leg
    }
    c.restore();           // Restore the transform
    c.translate(len, 0);   // Translate to end of leg
  }
}

// Draw snowflake fractals of level 0 through 4
snowflake(c,0,5,115,125);    // Equilateral triangle
snowflake(c,1,145,115,125);  // A 6-sided star
snowflake(c,2,285,115,125);  // Kind of a snowflake
snowflake(c,3,425,115,125);  // More snowflake-like
snowflake(c,4,565,115,125);  // This looks really fractal!
c.stroke();                  // Stroke this complicated path
```

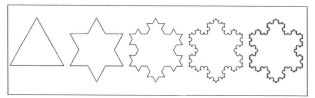

*Figure 1-5. Koch snowflakes*

# Drawing and Filling Curves

A path is a sequence of subpaths, and a subpath is a sequence of connected points. In the paths we defined in Examples 1-1 and 1-3, those points were connected with straight line segments, but that need not always be the case. The CanvasRenderingContext2D object defines a number of methods that add a new point to the subpath and connect the current point to that new point with a curve:

arc()

> This method adds an arc to the current subpath. It connects the current point to the beginning of the arc with a straight line, and then connects the beginning of the arc to the end of the arc with a portion of a circle, leaving the end of the arc as the new current point. The arc to be drawn is specified with six parameters: the X and Y coordinates of the center of a circle, the radius of the circle, the start and end angles of the arc, and the direction (clockwise or counterclockwise) of the arc between those two angles.

arcTo()

> This method draws a straight line and a circular arc just like the arc() method does, but specifies the arc to be drawn using different parameters. The arguments to arcTo() specify points P1 and P2 and a radius. The arc that is added to the path has the specified radius and is tangent to the line between the current point and P1, and also the line between P1 and P2. This unusual-seeming method of specifying arcs is actually quite useful for drawing shapes with rounded corners. If you specify a radius of 0, then this method just draws a straight line from the current point to P1. With a nonzero radius, however, it draws a straight line from the current point in the direction of P1, then curves that line around in a circle until it is heading in the direction of P2.

## bezierCurveTo()

This method adds a new point P to the subpath and connects it to the current point with a cubic Bézier curve. The shape of the curve is specified by two "control points" C1 and C2. At the start of the curve (at the current point), the curve heads in the direction of C1. At the end of the curve (at point P) the curve arrives from the direction of C2. In between these points the direction of the curve varies smoothly. The point P becomes the new current point for the subpath.

## quadraticCurveTo()

This method is like bezierCurveTo(), but it uses a quadratic Bézier curve instead of a cubic Bézier curve and has only a single control point.

You can use these methods to draw paths like those in Figure 1-6.

*Figure 1-6. Curved paths in a canvas*

Example 1-4 shows the code used to create Figure 1-6. The methods demonstrated in this code are some of the most complicated in the Canvas API; see the reference section for complete details on the methods and their arguments.

---

*Example 1-4. Adding curves to a path*

```
// A utility function to convert from degrees to radians
function rads(x) { return Math.PI*x/180; }


// Draw a circle. Scale and rotate if you want an ellipse
// instead. There is no current point, so this draws just
// the circle with no straight line from the current point
// to the start of the circle.
c.beginPath();
c.arc(75,100,50,              // Center at (75,100), radius 50
     0,rads(360),false);      // Go clockwise from 0 to 360°

// Draw a wedge. Angles are measured clockwise from the
// positive x axis. Note that arc() adds a line from the
// current point to the arc start.
c.moveTo(200, 100);           // Start at center of the circle
c.arc(200, 100, 50,           // Circle center and radius
     rads(-60), rads(0),      // start at -60° and go to 0°
     false);                  // false means clockwise
c.closePath();                // Go back to the circle center

// Same wedge, opposite direction
c.moveTo(325, 100);
c.arc(325, 100, 50, rads(-60), rads(0), true);
c.closePath();

// Use arcTo() for rounded corners. Here we draw a square
// with upper-left at (400,50) and various corner radii.
c.moveTo(450, 50);                 // Begin in middle of the top
c.arcTo(500,50,500,150,30);        // Top and upper-right corner
c.arcTo(500,150,400,150,20);       // Right and lower-right corner
c.arcTo(400,150,400,50,10);        // Bottom and lower-left corner
c.arcTo(400,50,500,50,0);          // Left and upper-left corner
c.closePath();                     // The rest of the top edge

// Quadratic Bezier curve: one control point
c.moveTo(75, 250);                        // Begin at (75,250)
c.quadraticCurveTo(100,200, 175, 250);    // Curve to (175,250)
c.fillRect(100-3,200-3,6,6);              // Mark the control point

// Cubic Bezier curve: two control points
c.moveTo(200, 250);                             // Start point
c.bezierCurveTo(220,220,280,280,300,250);       // To (300,250)
c.fillRect(220-3,220-3,6,6);              // Mark control points
c.fillRect(280-3,280-3,6,6);
```

```
// Define some graphics attributes and draw the curves
c.fillStyle = "#aaa";  // Gray fills
c.lineWidth = 5;       // 5-pixel black (by default) lines
c.fill();              // Fill the curves
c.stroke();            // Stroke their outlines
```

# Rectangles

CanvasRenderingContext2D defines four methods for drawing rectangles. Example 1-4 used one of them, `fillRect()`, to mark the control points of the Bézier curves. All four of these rectangle methods expect two arguments that specify one corner of the rectangle followed by the rectangle width and height. Normally, you specify the upper-left corner and then pass a positive width and positive height, but you may also specify other corners and pass negative dimensions.

`fillRect()` fills the specified rectangle with the current `fillStyle`. `strokeRect()` strokes the outline of the specified rectangle using the current `strokeStyle` and other line attributes. `clearRect(` is like `fillRect()`, but it ignores the current fill style and fills the rectangle with transparent black pixels (the default color of all blank canvases). The important thing about these three methods is that they do not affect the current path or the current point within that path.

The final rectangle method is named `rect()`, and it does affect the current path: it adds the specified rectangle, in a subpath of its own, to the path. Like other path-definition methods, it does not fill or stroke anything itself.

# Colors, Transparency, Gradients, and Patterns

The `strokeStyle` and `fillStyle` attributes specify how lines are stroked and regions are filled. Most often, these attributes are used to specify opaque or translucent colors, but you can also set them to CanvasPattern or CanvasGradient objects to stroke or fill with a repeated background image or with a linear or radial color gradient. In addition, you can set the `globalAlpha` property to make everything you draw translucent.

To specify a solid color, use one of the color names defined by the HTML4 standard,* or use a CSS color string:

```
context.strokeStyle = "blue"; // Stroke lines in blue
context.fillStyle = "#aaa";   // Fill with light gray
```

The default value for both `strokeStyle` and `fillStyle` is "#000000": opaque black.

Current browsers support CSS3 colors and allow the use of the RGB, RGBA, HSL, and HSLA color spaces in addition to basic hexadecimal RGB colors. Here are some example color strings:

```
"#f44"                   // Hexadecimal RGB value: red
"#44ff44"                // RRGGBB value: green
"rgb(60, 60, 255)"       // RGB as integers: blue
"rgb(100%, 25%, 100%)"   // RGB as percentages: purple
"rgba(100%,25%,100%,0.5)" // Plus alpha 0-1: translucent
"rgba(0,0,0,0)"          // Transparent black
"transparent"            // Synonym for the above
"hsl(60, 100%, 50%)"     // Fully saturated yellow
"hsl(60, 75%, 50%)"      // Less saturated yellow
"hsl(60, 100%, 75%)"     // Fully saturated, lighter
"hsl(60, 100%, 25%)"     // Fully saturated, darker
"hsla(60,100%,50%,0.5)"  // 50% opaque
```

The HSL color space specifies a color with three numbers that specify its hue, saturation, and lightness. Hue is an angle in degrees around a color wheel. A hue of 0 is red, 60 is yellow, 120 is green, 180 is cyan, 240 is blue, 300 is magenta, and 360 is back to red again. Saturation describes the intensity of the color, specified as a percentage. Colors with 0% saturation are shades of gray. Lightness describes how light or dark a color is and is also specified as a percentage. Any HSL color with 100% lightness is pure white and any color with 0% lightness is pure

---

* Aqua, black, blue, fuchsia, gray, green, lime, maroon, navy, olive, purple, red, silver, teal, white, and yellow

black. The HSLA color space is just like HSL, but adds an alpha value that ranges from 0.0 (transparent) to 1.0 (opaque).

If you want to work with translucent colors, but do not want to explicitly specify an alpha channel for each color, or if you want to add translucency to opaque images or patterns (for example) you can set the `globalAlpha` property. Every pixel you draw will have its alpha value multiplied by `globalAlpha`. The default is 1, which adds no transparency. If you set `globalAlpha` to 0, then everything you draw will be fully transparent and nothing will appear in the canvas. If you set this property to 0.5, then pixels that would otherwise have been opaque will be 50% opaque. And pixels that would have been 50% opaque will be 25% opaque instead. If you set `globalAlpha` to a value less than 1, then all your pixels will be translucent and you may have to consider how those pixels are combined (or "composited") with the pixels they are drawn over—see "Compositing" on page 39 for details about Canvas compositing modes.

Instead of drawing with solid (but possibly translucent) colors, you can also use color gradients and repeating images when filling and stroking paths. Figure 1-7 shows a rectangle stroked with wide lines and a patterned stroke style on top of a linear gradient fill and underneath a translucent radial gradient fill. The code fragments below show how the pattern and gradients were created.

To fill or stroke using a background image pattern instead of a color, set `fillStyle` or `strokeStyle` to the CanvasPattern object returned by the `createPattern()` method of the context object:

```
var image = document.getElementById("myimage");
c.fillStyle = c.createPattern(image, "repeat");
```

The first argument to `createPattern()` specifies the image to use as the pattern. It must be an `<img>`, `<canvas>`, or `<video>` element from the document (or an image object created with the `Image()` constructor). The second argument is typically "repeat" for a repeating image fill that is independent of the

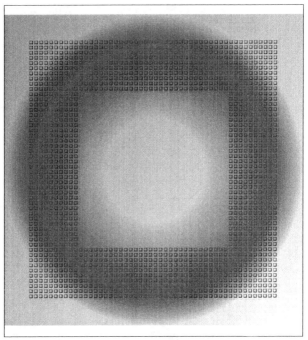

*Figure 1-7. Pattern and gradient fills*

size of the image, but you can also use "repeat-x", "repeat-y", or "no-repeat".

Note that you can use a `<canvas>` tag (even one that has never been added to the document and is not visible) as the pattern source for another `<canvas>`:

```
// Create an offscreen canvas and set its size
var offscreen = document.createElement("canvas");
offscreen.width = offscreen.height = 10;
// Get its context and draw into it
offscreen.getContext("2d").strokeRect(0,0,6,6);
// Use it as a pattern
var pattern = c.createPattern(offscreen,"repeat");
```

To fill (or stroke) with a color gradient, set `fillStyle` (or `strokeStyle`) to a CanvasGradient object returned by the `createLinearGradient()` or `createRadialGradient()` methods of the context. Creating gradients is a multistep process, and using them is trickier than using patterns.

The first step is to create the CanvasGradient object. The arguments to `createLinearGradient()` are the coordinates of two points that define a line (it does not need to be horizontal or vertical) along which the colors will vary. The arguments to `createRadialGradient()` specify the centers and radii of two circles. (They need not be concentric, but the first circle typically lies entirely inside the second.) Areas inside the smaller circle or outside the larger will be filled with solid colors: areas between the two will be filled with a color gradient.

After creating the CanvasGradient object and defining the regions of the canvas that will be filled, define the gradient colors by calling the `addColorStop()` method of the CanvasGradient. The first argument to this method is a number between 0.0 and 1.0. The second is a CSS color specification. You must call this method at least twice to define a simple color gradient, but you may call it more than that. The color at 0.0 will appear at the start of the gradient, and the color at 1.0 will appear at the end. If you specify additional colors, they will appear at the specified fractional position. Elsewhere, colors will be smoothly interpolated. Here are some examples:

```
// A linear gradient, diagonally across the canvas
// (assuming no transforms)
var bgfade = c.createLinearGradient(0,0,canvas.width,
                                    canvas.height);
// Start with light blue in upper-left and fade to
// white in lower-right
bgfade.addColorStop(0.0, "#88f");
bgfade.addColorStop(1.0, "#fff");

// A gradient between two concentric circles.
// Transparent in the middle, fading to translucent
// gray and then back to transparent.
var peekhole = c.createRadialGradient(300,300,100,
                                      300,300,300);
```

```
peekhole.addColorStop(0.0, "transparent");
peekhole.addColorStop(0.7, "rgba(100,100,100,.9)");
peekhole.addColorStop(1.0, "rgba(0,0,0,0)");
```

An important point to understand about gradients is that they
are not position-independent. When you create a gradient, you
specify bounds for the gradient. If you then attempt to fill an
area outside of those bounds you'll get the solid color defined
at one end or the other of the gradient. If you define a gradient
along the line between (0,0) and (100,100), for example, you
should only use that gradient to fill objects located within the
rectangle (0,0,100,100).

The graphic shown in Figure 1-7 was created with the code
below (using the **pattern** pattern and the **bgfade** and **peek
hole** gradients defined above):

```
c.fillStyle = bgfade;       // Use the linear gradient
c.fillRect(0,0,600,600);    // to fill the entire canvas.
c.strokeStyle = pattern;    // Use the pattern
c.lineWidth = 100;          // and really wide lines
c.strokeRect(100,100,       // to draw a big square.
             400,400);
c.fillStyle = peekhole;     // Use the translucent radial
c.fillRect(0,0,600,600);    // gradient to fill canvas.
```

# Line-Drawing Attributes

You've already seen the lineWidth property, which specifies the
width of the lines drawn by stroke() and strokeRect(). In addition to lineWidth (and strokeStyle, of course) there are three
other graphics attributes that affect line drawing.

The default value of the lineWidth property is 1, and you can
set it to any positive number, even fractional values less than
1. (Lines that are less than one pixel wide are drawn with
translucent colors, so they look less dark than 1-pixel-wide
lines). To fully understand the lineWidth property, it is important to visualize paths as infinitely thin one-dimensional lines.
The lines and curves drawn by the stroke() method are centered over the path, with half of the lineWidth on either side.
If you're stroking a closed path and only want the line to appear

outside the path, stroke the path first and then fill with an opaque color to hide the portion of the stroke that appears inside the path. Or if you only want the line to appear inside a closed path, call the save() and clip() methods (see "Clipping" on page 32) first and then call stroke() and restore().

Line widths are affected by the current transformation, as you may be able to make out in the scaled axes at the upper-right of Figure 1-4. If you call scale(2,1) to scale the X dimension and leave Y unaffected, then vertical lines will be twice as wide as horizontal lines drawn with the same lineWidth setting. It is important to understand that line width is determined by the lineWidth and the current transform at the time stroke() is called, not at the time that lineTo() or another path-building method is called.

The other three line-drawing attributes affect the appearance of the unconnected ends of paths and the vertices where two path segments meet. The have very little visual impact for narrow lines, but make a big difference when you are drawing with wide lines. Two of these properties are illustrated in Figure 1-8. The figure shows the path as a thin black line and the stroke as the gray area that surrounds it.

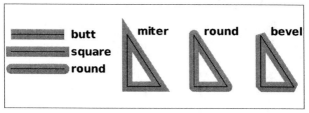

*Figure 1-8. The lineCap and lineJoin attributes*

The lineCap property specifies how the ends of an open sub-path are "capped." The value "butt" (the default) means that the line terminates abruptly at the endpoint. The value "square" means that the line extends, by half of the line width, beyond the endpoint. And the value "round" means that the line is extended with a half circle (of radius one-half the line width) beyond the endpoint.

The `lineJoin` property specifies how the vertices between sub-path segments are connected. The default value is "miter", which means that the outside edges of the two path segments are extended until they meet at a point. The value "round" means that the vertex is rounded off, and the value "bevel" means that the vertex is cut off with a straight line.

The final line-drawing property is `miterLimit`, which only applies when `lineJoin` is "miter". When two lines meet at a sharp angle, the miter between them can become quite long, and these long, jagged miters are visually distracting. The `miterLimit` property places an upper bound on miter length. If the miter at a given vertex would be longer than half of the line width times `miterLimit`, then that vertex will be drawn with a beveled join instead of a mitered join.

# Text

To draw text in a canvas, you normally use the `fillText()` method, which draws text using the color (or gradient or pattern) specified by the `fillStyle` property. For special effects at large text sizes, you can use `strokeText()` to draw the outline of the individual text glyphs (an example of outlined text appears in Figure 1-10). Both methods take the text to be drawn as their first argument and take the X and Y coordinates of the text as the second and third arguments. Neither method affects the current path or the current point. As you can see in Figure 1-4, text is affected by the current transformation.

The `font` property specifies the font to be used for text drawing. The value should be a string in the same syntax as the CSS `font` attribute. Some examples:

```
"48pt sans-serif"
"bold 18px Times Roman"
"italic 12pt monospaced"
// bolder and smaller than the <canvas> font
"bolder smaller serif"
```

The `textAlign` property specifies how the text should be horizontally aligned with respect to the X coordinate passed to `fillText()` or `strokeText()`. The `textBaseline` property specifies how the text should be vertically aligned with respect to the Y coordinate. Figure 1-9 illustrates the allowed values for these properties. The thin line near each string of text is the baseline, and the small square marks the point (x,y) that was passed to `fillText()`.

|  | start | left | center | right | end |
|---|---|---|---|---|---|
| top | Abcefg | Abcefg | Abcefg | Abcefg | Abcefg |
| hanging | Abcefg | Abcefg | Abcefg | Abcefg | Abcefg |
| middle | Abcefg | Abcefg | Abcefg | Abcefg | Abcefg |
| alphabetic | Abcefg | Abcefg | Abcefg | Abcefg | Abcefg |
| ideographic | Abcefg | Abcefg | Abcefg | Abcefg | Abcefg |
| bottom | Abcefg | Abcefg | Abcefg | Abcefg | Abcefg |

*Figure 1-9. The textAlign and textBaseline properties*

The default `textAlign` is "start". Note that for left-to-right text, an alignment of "start" is the same as "left" and an alignment of "end" is the same as "right". If you set the `dir` attribute of the `<canvas>` tag to "rtl" (right-to-left), however, then "start" alignment is the same as "right" alignment and "end" is the same as "left".

The default `textBaseline` is "alphabetic", and it is appropriate for Latin and similar scripts. The value "ideographic" is used with ideographic scripts such as Chinese and Japanese. The value "hanging" is intended for use with Devangari and similar scripts (which are used for many of the languages of India). The "top", "middle", and "bottom" baselines are purely geometric baselines, based on the "em square" of the font.

`fillText()` and `strokeText()` take an optional fourth argument. If specified, this argument specifies the maximum width of the text to be displayed. If the text would be wider than the specified value when drawn using the **font** property, then the canvas will make it fit by scaling it or by using a narrower or smaller font.

If you need to measure text yourself before drawing it, pass it to the **measureText()** method. This method returns a TextMetrics object that specifies the measurements of the text when drawn with the current **font**. At the time of this writing, the only "metric" contained in the **TextMetrics** object is the width. Query the onscreen width of a string like this:

```
var width = c.measureText(text).width;
```

# Clipping

After defining a path, you usually call **stroke()** or **fill()** (or both). You also call the **clip()** method to define a clipping region. Once a clipping region is defined, nothing will be drawn outside of it. Figure 1-10 shows a complex drawing produced using clipping regions. The vertical stripe running down the middle and the text along the bottom of the figure were stroked with no clipping region and then filled after the triangular clipping region was defined.

Figure 1-10 was generated using the **polygon()** method of Example 1-1 and the code of Example 1-5.

*Example 1-5. Defining a clipping region*

```
// Define some drawing attributes
c.font = "bold 60pt sans-serif";    // Big font
c.lineWidth = 2;                     // Narrow lines
c.strokeStyle = "#000";              // Black lines

// Outline a rectangle and some text
c.strokeRect(175, 25, 50, 325);      // Vertical stripe
c.strokeText("<canvas>", 15, 330);   // Text outline
```

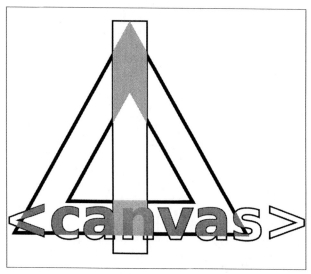

*Figure 1-10. Unclipped strokes and clipped fills*

```
// Define a complex path with an interior that is outside.
polygon(c,3,200,225,200);          // Large triangle
polygon(c,3,200,225,100,0,true);   // Small reverse triangle

// Make that path the clipping region.
c.clip();

// Stroke the path with a 5 pixel line,
// entirely inside the clipping region.
c.lineWidth = 10; // Half of this line will be clipped away
c.stroke();

// Fill the parts of the rectangle and text
// that are inside the clipping region
c.fillStyle = "#aaa"                // Light gray
c.fillRect(175, 25, 50, 325);       // Fill vertical stripe
c.fillStyle = "#888"                // Darker gray
c.fillText("<canvas>", 15, 330);    // Fill text
```

It is important to note that when you call **clip()**, the current path is itself clipped to the current clipping region, and then that clipped path becomes the new clipping region. This means that the `clip()` method can shrink the clipping region but can never enlarge it. There is no method to reset the clipping region, so before calling `clip()` you should typically call `save()` so that you can later `restore()` the unclipped region.

# Shadows

Four graphics attribute properties of the CanvasRendering-Context2D object control the drawing of drop shadows. If you set these properties appropriately, any line, area, text, or image you draw will be given a drop shadow, which will make it appear as if it is floating above the canvas surface. Figure 1-11 shows shadows beneath a filled rectangle, a stroked rectangle, and filled text.

*Figure 1-11. Automatically generated shadows*

The `shadowColor` property specifies the color of the shadow. The default is fully transparent black, and shadows will never

---

appear unless you set this property to a translucent or opaque color. This property can only be set to a color string: patterns and gradients are not allowed for shadows. Using a translucent shadow color produces the most realistic shadow effects because it allows the background to show through.

The shadowOffsetX and shadowOffsetY properties specify the X and Y offsets of the shadow. The default for both properties is 0, which places the shadow directly beneath your drawing, where it is not visible. If you set both properties to a positive value, then shadows will appear below and to the right of what you draw, as if there were a light source above and to the left shining onto the canvas from outside the computer screen. Larger offsets produce larger shadows and make drawn objects appear as if they are floating "higher" above the canvas.

The shadowBlur property specifies how blurred the edges of the shadow are. The default value is 0, which produces crisp, unblurred shadows. Larger values produce more blur, up to an implementation-defined upper bound. This property is a parameter to a Gaussian blur function and is not a size or length in pixels.

Example 1-6 shows the code used to produce Figure 1-11 and demonstrates each of these four shadow properties.

*Example 1-6. Setting shadow attributes*

```
// Define a subtle shadow
c.shadowColor = "rgba(100,100,100,.4)"; // Transparent gray
c.shadowOffsetX = c.shadowOffsetY = 3;  // Slight offset
c.shadowBlur = 5;                       // Soften edges

// Draw some text and a blue box using that shadow
c.lineWidth = 10;
c.strokeStyle = "blue";
c.strokeRect(100, 100, 300, 200);       // Draw a box
c.font = "Bold 36pt Helvetica";
c.fillText("Hello World", 115, 225);    // Draw some text

// Define a less subtle shadow. Larger offset makes items
// "float" higher. Note how the shadow overlaps the box.
c.shadowOffsetX = c.shadowOffsetY = 20; // Large offsets
```

```
c.shadowBlur = 10;                      // Softer edges
c.fillStyle = "red";        // Draw a solid red rectangle
c.fillRect(50,25,200,65); // that floats above the blue box
```

The shadowOffsetX and shadowOffsetY properties are always measured in the default coordinate space, and are not affected by the rotate() or scale() methods. Suppose, for example, that you rotate the coordinate system by 90 degrees to draw some vertical text and then restore the old coordinate system to draw horizontal text. Both the vertical and horizontal text will have shadows oriented in the same direction, which is what you probably want. Similarly, shapes drawn with different scaling transforms will still have shadows of the same "height."[†]

# Images

In addition to vector graphics (paths, lines, etc.) the Canvas API also supports bitmap images. The drawImage() method copies the pixels of a source image (or of a rectangle within the source image) onto the canvas, scaling and rotating the pixels of the image as necessary.

drawImage() can be invoked with three, five, or nine arguments. In all cases, the first argument is the source image from which pixels are to be copied. This image argument is often an <img> element, or an offscreen image created with the Image() constructor, but it can also be another <canvas> element or even a <video> element. If you specify an <img> or <video> tag that is still loading its data, the drawImage() call will do nothing.

In the three-argument version of drawImage(), the second and third arguments specify the X and Y coordinates at which the upper-left corner of the image is to be drawn. In this version of

---

† At the time of this writing, Google's Chrome browser gets this wrong, and transforms the shadow offsets.

the method, the entire source image is copied to the canvas. The X and Y coordinates are interpreted in the current coordinate system and the image is scaled and rotated if necessary.

The five-argument version of `drawImage()` adds *width* and *height* arguments to the *x* and *y* arguments described above. These four arguments define a destination rectangle within the canvas. The upper-left corner of the source image goes at `(x,y)` and the lower-right corner goes at `(x+width, y+height)`. Again, the entire source image is copied. The destination rectangle is measured in the current coordinate system. With this version of the method, the source image will be scaled to fit the destination rectangle even if no scaling transform has ever been specified.

The nine-argument version of `drawImage()` specifies both a source rectangle and a destination rectangle and copies only the pixels within the source rectangle. Arguments two through five specify the source rectangle. They are measured in CSS pixels. If the source image is another canvas the source rectangle uses the default coordinate system for that canvas, and ignores any transformations that have been specified. Arguments six through nine specify the destination rectangle into which the image is drawn and are in the current coordinate system of the canvas, not in the default coordinate system.

Example 1-7 is a simple demonstration of `drawImage()`. It uses the nine-argument version to copy pixels from a portion of a canvas and draw them, enlarged and rotated back onto the same canvas. As you can see in Figure 1-12, the image is enlarged enough to be pixelated, and you can see the translucent pixels used to smooth the edges of the line.

*Example 1-7. Using drawImage()*

```
// Draw a line in the upper left
c.moveTo(5,5);
c.lineTo(45,45);
c.lineWidth = 8;
c.lineCap = "round";
c.stroke();
```

```
// Define a transformation
c.translate(50,100);
c.rotate(-45*Math.PI/180); // Straighten out the line
c.scale(10,10);            // Scale so we can see the pixels

// Use drawImage() to copy the line
c.drawImage(c.canvas,      // Copy from canvas to itself
           0, 0, 50, 50,   // untransformed source rectangle
           0, 0, 50, 50);  // transformed destination
```

*Figure 1-12. Pixels enlarged with drawImage()*

In addition to drawing images into a canvas, we can also extract the content of a canvas as an image using the toDataURL() method. Unlike all the other methods described here, toDataURL() is a method of the Canvas element itself, not of the CanvasRenderingContext2D object. You normally invoke toDataURL() with no arguments, and it returns the content of the canvas as a PNG image, encoded as a string using a data: URL. The returned URL is suitable for use with an <img> tag, and you can make a static snapshot of a canvas with code like this:

```
// Create an <img> tag
var img = document.createElement("img");
// Set its src attribute
img.src = canvas.toDataURL();
// Append it to the document
document.body.appendChild(img);
```

All browsers are required to support the PNG image format. Some implementations may support other formats as well, and you can specify the desired MIME type with the optional first argument to toDataURL(). See the reference page for details.

There is one important security restriction you must be aware of when using toDataURL(). To prevent cross-origin information leaks, `toDataURL()` does not work on `<canvas>` tags that are not "origin-clean." A canvas is not origin-clean if it has ever had an image drawn in it (directly by `drawImage()` or indirectly through a CanvasPattern) that has a different origin than the document that contains the canvas.

# Compositing

When you stroke lines, fill regions, draw text, or copy images, you expect the new pixels to be drawn on top of the pixels that are already in the canvas. If you are drawing opaque pixels, then they simply replace the pixels that are already there. If you are drawing with translucent pixels, then the new ("source") pixel is combined with the old ("destination") pixel so that the old pixel shows through the new pixel based on how transparent that pixel is.

This process of combining new translucent source pixels with existing destination pixels is called *compositing*, and the compositing process described above is the default way that the Canvas API combines pixels. You don't always want compositing to happen, however. Suppose you've drawn into a canvas using translucent pixels and now want to make a temporary alteration to the canvas and then restore it to its original state. An easy way to do this is to copy your drawing to an offscreen canvas using `drawImage()`. Then, when it is time to restore the canvas, you can copy your pixels from the offscreen canvas in which you saved them back to the onscreen canvas. Remember, though, that the pixels you saved were translucent. If compositing is on they won't fully obscure and erase the temporary drawing you've done. In this scenario, you need a way to turn compositing off: to draw the source pixels and ignore the destination pixels regardless of the transparency of the source.

To specify the kind of compositing to be done, set the `global CompositeOperation` property. The default value is "source-over" which means that source pixels are drawn "over" the destination pixels and are combined with them if the source is translucent. If you set this property to "copy", then compositing is turned off: source pixels are copied to the canvas unchanged and destination pixels are ignored (but see the discussion below about implementation differences in the definition of source pixels). Another `globalCompositeOperation` value that is sometimes useful is "destination-over". This kind of compositing combines pixels as if the new source pixels were drawn beneath the existing destination pixels. If the destination is translucent or transparent then some or all of the source pixel color is visible in the resulting color.

"source-over", "destination-over", and "copy" are three of the most commonly used types of compositing, but the Canvas API supports 11 values for the `globalCompositeOperation` attribute. The names of these compositing operations are suggestive of what they do, and you can go a long way toward understanding compositing by combining the operation names with visual examples of how they work. Figure 1-13 illustrates all 11 operations using "hard" transparency: all the pixels involved are fully opaque or fully transparent. In each of the 11 boxes, the square is drawn first and serves as the destination. Next `globalCompositeOperation` is set, and the circle is drawn as the source.

Figure 1-14 is a similar example that uses "soft" transparency. In this version the square and circle are drawn using radial gradients so that they have an opaque perimeter and a translucent center.

You may find that it is not so easy to understand the compositing operations when used with translucent pixels like these. If you are interested in a deeper understanding, the reference page for `globalCompositeOperation` includes the equations that specify how individual pixel values are computed from source and destination pixels for each of the 11 compositing operations.

At the time of this writing, browser vendors disagree on the implementation of 5 of the 11 compositing modes: "copy",

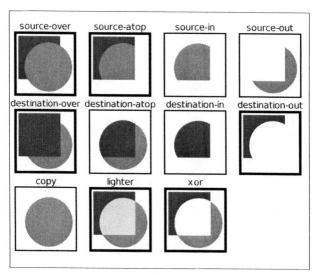

*Figure 1-13. Compositing operations with hard transparency*

"source-in", "source-out", "destination-atop", and "destination-in" behave differently in different browsers and cannot be used portably. A detailed explanation follows, but you can skip to the next section if you don't plan on using any of these compositing operations.

The five compositing modes listed above either ignore the destination pixel values in the computation of result pixels or make the result transparent anywhere the source is transparent. The difference in implementation has to do with the definition of the source pixels. Safari and Chrome perform compositing "locally": only the pixels actually drawn by the `fill()`, `stroke()`, or other drawing operation count as part of the source. IE 9 is likely to follow suit. Firefox and Opera perform compositing "globally": every pixel within the current clipping region is composited for every drawing operation. If the source does not set that pixel, then it is treated as transparent black. In Firefox and Opera this means that the five compositing modes listed above actually erase destination pixels outside of

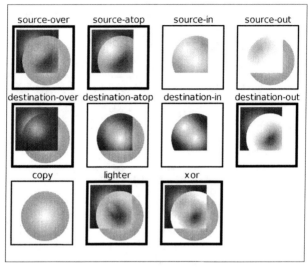

*Figure 1-14. Compositing operations with soft transparency*

the source and inside the clipping region. Figures 1-13 and 1-14 were generated in Firefox, and this is why the boxes around "copy", "source-in", "source-out", "destination-atop", and "destination-in" are thinner than the other boxes: the rectangle around each sample is the clipping region and these four compositing operations erase the portion of the stroke (half of the lineWidth) that falls inside the path. For comparison, Figure 1-15 shows the same images as Figure 1-14, but was generated in Chrome.

The HTML5 draft current at the time of this writing specifies the global compositing approach implemented by Firefox and Opera. Browser vendors are aware of the incompatibility and are not satisfied with the current state of the specification. There is a distinct possibility that the specification will be altered to require local compositing instead of global compositing.

---

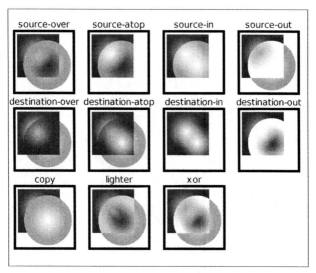

*Figure 1-15. Compositing locally rather than globally*

Finally, note that it is possible to perform global compositing in browsers like Safari and Chrome that implement local compositing. First, create a blank offscreen canvas of the same dimensions as the onscreen canvas. Then draw your source pixels into the offscreen canvas and use `drawImage()` to copy the offscreen pixels to the onscreen canvas and composite them globally within the clipping region. There is not a general technique for performing local compositing in browsers like Firefox that implement global compositing, but you can often come close by defining an appropriate clipping region before performing the drawing operation that is to be locally composited.

# Pixel Manipulation

The `getImageData()` method returns an ImageData object that represents the raw (nonpremultiplied) pixels (as R, G, B, and A components) from a rectangular region of your canvas.

You can create empty blank `ImageData` objects with `createImageData()`. The pixels in an ImageData object are writable, so you can set them any way you want, and then copy those pixels back onto the canvas with `putImageData()`.

These pixel manipulation methods provide very low-level access to the canvas. The rectangle you pass to `getImageData()` is in the default coordinate system: its dimensions are measured in CSS pixels, and it is not affected by the current transformation. When you call `putImageData()`, the position you specify is also measured in the default coordinate system. Furthermore, `putImageData()` ignores all graphics attributes. It does not perform any compositing, it does not multiply pixels by `globalAlpha`, and it does not draw shadows.

Pixel manipulation methods are useful for implementing image processing. Example 1-8 shows how to create a simple motion blur or "smear" effect on the graphics in a canvas. The example demonstrates `getImageData()` and `putImageData()` and shows how to iterate through and modify the pixel values in an ImageData object, but it does not explain these things in any detail. See the CanvasRenderingContext2D reference pages for complete details on `getImageData()` and `putImageData()` and see the ImageData reference page for details on that object.

*Example 1-8. Motion blur with ImageData*

```
// Smear the pixels of the rectangle to the right, producing
// a sort of motion blur as if objects are moving from right
// to left. n must be 2 or larger. Larger values produce
// bigger smears. The rectangle is specified in the default
// coordinate system.
function smear(c, n, x, y, w, h) {
    // Get the ImageData object that represents the
    // rectangle of pixels to smear
    var pixels = c.getImageData(x,y,w,h);

    // This smear is done in-place and requires only the
    // source ImageData. Some image processing algorithms
    // require an additional ImageData to store transformed
    // pixel values. If we needed an output buffer, we could
    // create a new ImageData with the same dimensions like
    // this: var output_pixels = c.createImageData(pixels);
```

```
    // These dimensions may be different than the w and h
    // arguments: there may be more than one device pixel
    // per CSS pixel.
    var width = pixels.width, height = pixels.height;

    // This is the byte array that holds the raw pixel data,
    // left-to-right and top-to-bottom. Each pixel occupies
    // 4 consecutive bytes in R,G,B,A order.
    var data = pixels.data;

    // Each pixel after the first in each row is smeared by
    // replacing it with 1/nth of its own value plus m/nths
    // of the previous pixel's value
    var m = n-1;

    for(var row = 0; row < height; row++) { // For each row
        // Compute offset of the second pixel of the row
        var i = row*width*4 + 4;
        // For each pixel in the row, starting at the second
        for(var col = 1; col < width; col++, i += 4) {
            data[i] =   (data[i]+data[i-4]*m)/n;   // Red
            data[i+1] = (data[i+1]+data[i-3]*m)/n; // Green
            data[i+2] = (data[i+2]+data[i-2]*m)/n; // Blue
            data[i+3] = (data[i+3]+data[i-1]*m)/n; // Alpha
        }
    }

    // Now copy the smeared image data back to the canvas
    c.putImageData(pixels, x, y);
}
```

Note that getImageData() is subject to the same cross-origin
security restriction that the toDataURL() is: it does not work on
any canvas that has ever had an image drawn in it (directly by
drawImage() or indirectly through a CanvasPattern) that has a
different origin than the document that contains the canvas.

# Hit Detection

The method isPointInPath() determines whether a specified
point falls within (or on the boundary of) the current path, and
returns true if so or false otherwise. The point you pass to the

method is in the default coordinate system and is not transformed. This makes this method useful for *hit detection*: determining whether a mouse click occurred over a particular shape.

You can't pass the **clientX** and **clientY** fields of a MouseEvent object directly to **isPointInPath()**, however. First, the mouse event coordinates must be translated to be relative to the canvas element rather than the Window object. Second, if the onscreen size of the canvas is different than its actual dimensions, the mouse event coordinates must be scaled appropriately. Example 1-9 shows a utility function you can use to determine whether a given MouseEvent was over the current path.

*Example 1-9. Testing whether a mouse event is over the current path*

```
// Returns true if the mouse event is over the current path
// in the specified CanvasRenderingContext2D object.
function hitpath(context, event) {
    var canvas, bb, x, y;

    // Get <canvas> element from the context object
    canvas = context.canvas;

    // Get canvas size and position
    bb = canvas.getBoundingClientRect();

    // Convert mouse event coordinates to canvas coordinates
    x = (event.clientX-bb.left) * (canvas.width/bb.width);
    y = (event.clientY-bb.top) * (canvas.height/bb.height);

    // Call isPointInPath with these transformed coordinates
    return context.isPointInPath(x,y);
}
```

You might use this **hitpath()** function in an event handler like this:

```
    canvas.onclick = function(event) {
        if (hitpath(this.getContext("2d"), event)) {
            alert("Hit!");  // Click over current path
        }
    };
```

Instead of doing path-based hit detection, you can use getImageData() to test whether the pixel under the mouse point has been painted. If the returned pixel (or pixels) are fully transparent then nothing has been drawn into that pixel and the mouse event is a miss. Example 1-10 shows how you can do this kind of hit detection.

*Example 1-10. Testing whether a mouse event is over a painted pixel*

```
// Returns true if the specified mouse event is over a
// nontransparent pixel.
function hitpaint(context, event) {
    // Convert mouse event coordinates to canvas coordinates
    var canvas = context.canvas;
    var bb = canvas.getBoundingClientRect();
    var x=(event.clientX-bb.left)*(canvas.width/bb.width);
    var y=(event.clientY-bb.top)*(canvas.height/bb.height);

    // Get the pixel (or pixels if multiple device pixels
    // map to 1 CSS pixel) at those coordinates
    var pixels = c.getImageData(x,y,1,1);

    // If any pixels have a nonzero alpha, return true
    for(var i = 3; i < pixels.data.length; i+=4) {
        if (pixels.data[i] !== 0) return true;
    }

    // Otherwise it was a miss.
    return false;
}
```

# Canvas Example: Sparklines

We'll end this chapter with a practical example for drawing sparklines. A *sparkline* is a small data-display graphic intended to be included within the flow of text, like this one: Server load: ‸‸‸ 8. The term "sparkline" was coined by author Edward Tufte, who describes them as "small, high-resolution graphics embedded in a context of words, numbers, images. Sparklines are data-intense, design-simple, word-sized graphics." Learn more about sparklines in Tufte's book *Beautiful Evidence* (Graphics Press).

Example 1-11 is a relatively simple module of unobtrusive
JavaScript code for enabling sparklines in your web pages. The
comments explain how it works.

*Example 1-11. Sparklines with the <canvas> tag*

```
/*
 * Find all elements of CSS class "sparkline", parse their
 * content as a series of numbers, and replace it with a
 * graphical representation.
 *
 * Define sparklines with markup like this:
 *    <span class="sparkline">3 5 7 6 6 9 11 15</span>
 *
 * Style sparklines with CSS like this:
 *    .sparkline { background-color: #ddd; color: red; }
 *
 * - Sparkline color is from the computed style of the CSS
 *   color property.
 * - Sparklines are transparent, so the normal background
 *   color shows through.
 * - Sparkline height is from the data-height attribute if
 *   defined or from the computed style for the font-size
 *   otherwise.
 * - Sparkline width is from the data-width attribute if it
 *   is defined or the number of data points times data-dx
 *   if that is defined or the number of data points times
 *   the height divided by 6
 * - The minimum and maximum values of the y axis are taken
 *   from the data-ymin and data-ymax attributes if they
 *   are defined, and otherwise come from the minimum and
 *   maximum values of the data.
 */
// Run this code when the document first loads
window.addEventListener("load", function() {
    // Find all elements of class "sparkline"
    var elts = document.getElementsByClassName("sparkline");
    // Loop through those elements
    main: for(var e = 0; e < elts.length; e++) {
        var elt = elts[e];

        // Get content of the element and convert to an
        // array of numbers.  If the conversion fails, skip
        // this element.
        var content = elt.textContent || elt.innerText;
        // Trim leading and trailing whitespace
```

```javascript
var content = content.replace(/^\s+|\s+$/g, "");
// Remove comments
var text = content.replace(/#.*$/gm, "");
// Convert newlines, etc., to spaces
text = text.replace(/[\n\r\t\v\f]/g, " ");
// Split numbers on commas or spaces
var data = text.split(/\s+|\s*,\s*/);
// For each split piece of the string
for(var i = 0; i < data.length; i++) {
    data[i] = Number(data[i]); // Convert to number
    if (isNaN(data[i]))        // On failure
        continue main;         // skip this elt.
}

// Now compute the color, width, height, and y axis
// bounds of the sparkline from the data, from data-
// attributes of the element, and from the computed
// style of the element
var style = getComputedStyle(elt, null);
var color = style.color;
var height =
    parseInt(elt.getAttribute("data-height")) ||
    parseInt(style.fontSize) || 20;
var datadx = parseInt(elt.getAttribute("data-dx"));
var width =
    parseInt(elt.getAttribute("data-width")) ||
    data.length*(datadx || height/6);
var ymin =
    parseInt(elt.getAttribute("data-ymin")) ||
    Math.min.apply(Math, data);
var ymax =
    parseInt(elt.getAttribute("data-ymax")) ||
    Math.max.apply(Math, data);
if (ymin >= ymax) ymax = ymin + 1;

// Create the canvas element
var canvas = document.createElement("canvas");
canvas.width = width;     // Set canvas dimensions
canvas.height = height;
// Use the element content as a tooltip
canvas.title = content;
elt.innerHTML = "";       // Erase existing content
elt.appendChild(canvas); // Insert canvas into elt

// Now plot the points in the canvas
var context = canvas.getContext('2d');
for(var i = 0; i < data.length; i++) {
```

```
            // Transform (i,data[i]) to canvas coordinates
            var x = width*i/data.length;
            var y = (ymax-data[i])*height/(ymax-ymin);
            // Draw a line to (x,y). Note that the first
            // call to lineTo() does a moveTo() instead.
            context.lineTo(x,y);
        }
        context.strokeStyle = color; // Specify color
        context.stroke();            // and draw it
    }
}, false);  // last argument to addEventListener()
```

# CHAPTER 2

# Canvas Reference

This part of the book is a reference section that covers the `<canvas>` tag and its related classes. The reference is arranged alphabetically and methods are alphabetized by their full names, which include the names of the classes that define them. If you want to read about the `getContext()` method, for example, you'd look up `Canvas.getContext()`. And if you want to read about the `arc()` method, you'd look up `CanvasRenderingContext2D.arc()`. Because the name of that class is so long, however, it is abbreviated as CRC in this reference.

Most of this chapter documents methods of Canvas RenderingContext2D (using the name CRC), but Canvas, CanvasGradient, CanvasPattern, ImageData, and TextMetrics are also covered.

---

## Canvas                                    an HTML element for scripted drawing

### Properties

`String width, height`
> These properties mirror the `width` and `height` attributes of the `<canvas>` tag and specify the dimensions of the canvas coordinate space. The defaults are 300 for `width` and 150 for `height`.

---

If the size of the canvas element is not otherwise specified in a stylesheet or with the inline `style` attribute, then these `width` and `height` properties also specify the onscreen dimensions of the canvas element.

Setting either of these properties (even setting one to its current value) clears the canvas to transparent black and resets all of its graphics attributes to their default values.

## Methods

getContext()

Returns a context object with which you can draw on the canvas. Pass the string "2d" to obtain a CanvasRenderingContext2D that allows two-dimensional drawing.

Pass the string "webgl" to obtain a WebGLRenderingContext object for 3D rendering in browsers that support it. WebGL-RenderingContext is not yet standardized and is not documented in this book.

toDataURL()

Returns a `data:` URL representing the image on the canvas.

## Description

The Canvas object represents an HTML canvas element. It has no behavior of its own but defines an API that supports scripted client-side drawing operations. You may specify the `width` and `height` directly on this object, and can extract an image from the canvas with `toDataURL()`, but the actual drawing API is implemented by a separate "context" object returned by the `getContext()` method. See CRC.

The <canvas> tag was introduced in Safari 1.3 and is being standardized in HTML5. It is well supported in all recent versions of Firefox, Safari, Chrome, and Opera. Canvas will be supported in Internet Explorer 9, and can be emulated in earlier versions of IE using the open source ExplorerCanvas library at *http://code.google .com/p/explorercanvas/*.

## See Also

CRC

---

# Canvas.getContext()  returns a context for drawing on the canvas

## Synopsis

    Object getContext(String contextID)

## Arguments

*contextID*

> This argument specifies the type of drawing you want to do with the canvas. Pass the string "2d" to obtain a CanvasRenderingContext2D object with which you can do two-dimensional drawing.

## Returns

An object with which you can draw into the Canvas element. When you pass the string "2d", this will be a CanvasRenderingContext2D object for 2D drawing.

## Description

There is only one CanvasRenderingContext2D object per canvas element, so repeated calls to getContext("2d") return the same object.

HTML5 standardizes the "2d" argument to this method and defines no other valid arguments. A separate standard, WebGL, is under development for 3D graphics. In browsers that support it, you can pass the string "webgl" to this method to obtain an object that allows 3D rendering. Note, however, that the CanvasRenderingContext2D object is the only drawing context documented in this book.

## See Also

CRC

---

# Canvas.toDataURL()  returns canvas image as a data: URL

## Synopsis

    String toDataURL()
    String toDataURL(String type, parameters...)

---

Canvas.toDataURL()

## Arguments

*type*

> A string specifying the MIME type of the image format to use. If this argument is omitted, the default value is "image/png", and the PNG image format is the only one that implementations are required to support.

*parameters...*

> For image types other than PNG, additional arguments may be specified that provide encoding details. If *type* is "image/jpeg", for example, then the second argument should be a number between 0 and 1 specifying the image quality level. No other parameter arguments are standardized at the time of this writing.

## Returns

A string, containing a PNG representation of the canvas bitmap, encoded as a data: URL

## Description

toDataURL() returns the contents of the canvas bitmap in a URL form that can easily be used with an <img> tag or transmitted across the network.

To prevent cross-origin information leaks, toDataURL() does not work on <canvas> tags that are not "origin-clean." A canvas is not origin-clean if it has ever had an image drawn in it (directly by drawImage() or indirectly through a CanvasPattern) that has a different origin than the document that contains the canvas.

## Example

```
// Copy the content of a canvas to an image element
// and append that image to the document
var canvas = document.getElementById("my_canvas");
var image = document.createElement("img");
image.src = canvas.toDataURL();
document.body.appendChild(image);
```

## See Also

CRC.getImageData()

---

## CanvasGradient a color gradient for use in a canvas

### Methods

addColorStop()
> Specifies a color and position for the gradient

### Description

A CanvasGradient object represents a color gradient that may be assigned to both the strokeStyle and fillStyle properties of a CanvasRenderingContext2D object. The createLinearGradient() and createRadialGradient() methods of CanvasRenderingContext2D both return CanvasGradient objects.

Once you have created a CanvasGradient object, use addColorStop() to specify what colors should appear at what positions within the gradient. Between the positions you specify, colors are interpolated to create a smooth gradient or fade. If you specify no color stops, the gradient will be uniform transparent black.

### See Also

CRC.createLinearGradient(), CRC.createRadialGradient()

---

## CanvasGradient.addColorStop() specifies a color in the gradient

### Synopsis

```
void addColorStop(float offset, String color)
```

### Arguments

offset
> A floating-point value in the range 0.0 to 1.0 that represents a fraction between the start and endpoints of the gradient. An offset of 0 corresponds to the start point, and an offset of 1 corresponds to the endpoint.

color
> Specifies the color to be displayed at the specified offset, as a CSS color string. Colors at other points along the gradient are interpolated based on this and any other color stops.

## Description

addColorStop() specifies fixed colors within a gradient. If you specify two or more color stops, the gradient will smoothly interpolate colors between the stops. Before the first stop, the gradient will display the color of the first stop. After the last stop, the gradient will display the color of the last stop. If you specify only a single stop, the gradient will be one solid color. If you specify no color stops, the gradient will be uniform transparent black.

---

# CanvasPattern                    an image-based pattern for use in a canvas

## Description

A CanvasPattern object is returned by the createPattern() method of a CanvasRenderingContext2D object. A CanvasPattern object may be used as the value of the strokeStyle and fillStyle properties of a CanvasRenderingContext2D object.

A CanvasPattern object has no properties or methods of its own. See CRC.createPattern() for details on how to create one.

## See Also

CRC.createPattern()

---

# CanvasPixelArray                                           see ImageData

---

# CRC                          the rendering context for drawing on a canvas

## Properties

readonly Canvas canvas
    The Canvas element upon which this context will draw.

Object fillStyle
    The current color, pattern, or gradient used for filling paths. This property may be set to a CSS color string or to a CanvasGradient or CanvasPattern object. The default fill style is solid black. See also CRC.createLinearGradient(), CRC.createRadialGradient(), and CRC.createPattern().

---

String font
> The font to be used by text-drawing methods, specified as a string, using the same syntax as the CSS font attribute. The default is "10px sans-serif". If the font string uses font size units like "em" or "ex" or uses relative keywords like "larger", "smaller", "bolder", or "lighter", then these are interpreted relative to the computed style of the CSS font of the <canvas> element.

float globalAlpha
> Specifies additional transparency to be added to everything drawn on the canvas. The alpha value of all pixels drawn on the canvas is multiplied by the value of this property. The value must be a number between 0.0 (makes everything completely transparent) and 1.0 (the default: adds no additional transparency).

String globalCompositeOperation
> Specifies how colors being drawn are combined (or "composited") with colors already on the canvas. See the individual reference entry for this property for possible values. The default value is "source-over".

String lineCap
> Specifies how the ends of lines are rendered. Legal values are "butt", "round", and "square". The default is "butt". See the individual reference page for this property for further details.

String lineJoin
> Specifies how two lines are joined. Legal values are "round", "bevel", and "miter". The default is "miter". See the individual reference page for this property for further details.

float lineWidth
> Specifies the line width for stroking (line-drawing) operations. The default is 1. Lines are centered over the path, with half of the line width on each side.

float miterLimit
> When the lineJoin property is "miter", this property specifies the maximum ratio of miter length to half the line width. The default is 10. See the individual reference page for this property for further details.

String textAlign

> Specifies the horizontal alignment of text and the meaning of the X coordinate passed to fillText() and strokeText(). Legal values are "left", "center", "right", "start", and "end". The meaning of "start" and "end" depend on the dir (text direction) attribute of the <canvas> tag. The default is "start".

String textBaseline

> Specifies the vertical alignment of text and the meaning of the Y coordinate passed to fillText() and strokeText(). Legal values are "top", "middle", "bottom", "alphabetic", "hanging", and "ideographic". The default is "alphabetic".

float shadowBlur

> Specifies how much blur shadows should have. The default is 0, which produces crisp-edged shadows. Larger values produce larger blurs, but note that the units are not measured in pixels and are not affected by the current transform.

String shadowColor

> Specifies the color of shadows as a CSS color string. The default is transparent black.

float shadowOffsetX, shadowOffsetY

> Specifies the horizontal and vertical offset of the shadows. Larger values make the shadowed object appear to float higher above the background. The default is 0. These values are in coordinate space units and they are independent of the current transform.

Object strokeStyle

> Specifies the color, pattern, or gradient used for stroking (drawing) paths. This property may be a CSS color string, or a CanvasGradient or a CanvasPattern object. See also CRC.createLinearGradient(), CRC.createRadialGradient(), and CRC.createPattern().

## Methods

arc()

> Adds a line and a portion of a circle to the current subpath, using a center point and radius.

arcTo()

> Adds a line and a portion of a circle to the current subpath, using a radius and two lines tangent to the circle. Typically used for drawing rounded corners.

beginPath()

> Starts a new path (or a collection of subpaths) in a canvas.

bezierCurveTo()

> Adds a cubic Bézier curve to the current subpath.

clearRect()

> Erases the pixels in a rectangular area of a canvas.

clip()

> Uses the current path as the clipping region for subsequent drawing operations.

closePath()

> Closes the current subpath, connecting the current point to the initial point of the subpath.

createImageData()

> Returns a new ImageData object, representing a rectangular array of RGBA pixels, all initialized to transparent black.

createLinearGradient()

> Returns a CanvasGradient object that represents a linear color gradient.

createPattern()

> Returns a CanvasPattern object that represents a tiled image.

createRadialGradient()

> Returns a CanvasGradient object that represents a radial color gradient.

drawImage()

> Copies an image onto the canvas.

fill()

> Fills the interior of the current path with the color, gradient, or pattern specified by the fillStyle property.

fillRect()

> Fills the specified rectangle.

CRC

**fillText()**

Draws the specified text at the specified position using the current fillStyle.

**getImageData()**

Returns an ImageData object that holds the pixel values for a rectangular region of the canvas.

**isPointInPath()**

Tests whether a specified point falls within the currently defined path.

**lineTo()**

Adds a straight line segment to the current subpath.

**measureText()**

Returns a TextMetrics object that describes the size of the specified text. Currently, TextMetrics contains only the width of the text.

**moveTo()**

Sets the current position and begins a new subpath.

**putImageData()**

Copies some or all of the pixels in an ImageData object into a rectangular region of the canvas.

**quadraticCurveTo()**

Adds a quadratic Bézier curve to the current subpath.

**rect()**

Adds a rectangle subpath to the current path.

**restore()**

Resets the canvas to the graphics state most recently saved.

**rotate()**

Adds a rotation to the current transformation matrix.

**save()**

Saves the properties, clipping region, and transformation matrix of the CRC object.

**scale()**

Adds a scaling operation to the current transformation matrix.

`setTransform()`
> Sets the current transformation matrix.

`stroke()`
> Draws, or strokes, a line following the current path. The line is drawn according to the `lineWidth`, `lineJoin`, `lineCap`, `miter Limit` and `strokeStyle` properties.

`strokeRect()`
> Draws (but does not fill) a rectangle.

`strokeText()`
> Strokes the outline of the specified text at the specified position, using the current `strokeStyle`. For ordinary solid text, use `fillText()` instead.

`transform()`
> Multiplies the current transformation matrix by the specified matrix.

`translate()`
> Adds a translation to the current transformation matrix.

## Description

The CRC object provides properties and methods for drawing two-dimensional graphics. CRC is an abbreviation used in this reference section: the full name of this class is CanvasRenderingContext2D. The following sections provide an overview of the drawing API that the CRC defines.

### Creating and rendering paths

A powerful feature of the canvas is its ability to build shapes up from basic drawing operations, then either draw their outlines (*stroke* them) or paint their contents (*fill* them). The operations accumulated are collectively referred to as the *current path*. A canvas maintains a single current path.

In order to build a connected shape out of multiple segments, a joining point is needed between drawing operations. For this purpose, the canvas maintains a *current position*. The canvas drawing operations implicitly use this as their start point and update it to what is typically their endpoint. You can think of this like drawing with a pen on paper: when finishing a particular line or curve, the current position is where the pen rested after completing the operation.

You can create a sequence of disconnected shapes in the current path that will be rendered together with the same drawing parameters. To separate shapes, use the moveTo() method; this moves the current position to a new location without adding a connecting line. When you do this, you create a new *subpath*, which is the canvas term used for a collection of operations that are connected.

The available path operations are lineTo() for drawing straight lines, rect() for drawing rectangles, arc() and arcTo() for drawing partial circles, and bezierCurveTo() and quadraticCurveTo() for drawing curves. See "Drawing Lines and Filling Polygons" on page 5 and "Drawing and Filling Curves" on page 20 for more on these methods.

Once the path is complete, you can draw its outline with stroke(), paint its contents with fill(), or do both.

In addition to stroking and filling, you can also use the current path to specify the *clipping region* the canvas uses when rendering. Pixels inside this region are displayed; those outside are not. The clipping region is cumulative; calling clip() intersects the current path with the current clipping region to yield a new region. See "Clipping" on page 32 for more.

If the segments in any of the subpaths do not form a closed shape, fill() and clip() operations implicitly close them for you by adding a virtual (not visible with a stroke) line segment from the start to the end of the subpath. Optionally, you can call closePath() to explicitly add this line segment.

To test whether a point is inside (or on the boundary of) the current path, use isPointInPath(). (See also "Hit Detection" on page 45.) When a path intersects itself or consists of multiple overlapping subpaths, the definition of "inside" is based on the nonzero winding rule. If you draw a circle inside another circle, and both circles are drawn in the same direction, then everything inside the larger circle is considered inside the path. If, on the other hand, one circle is drawn clockwise and the other counterclockwise, then you have defined a donut shape, and the interior of the smaller circle is outside of the path. This same definition of insideness is used by the fill() and clip() methods.

### Colors, gradients, and patterns

When filling or stroking paths, you can specify how the lines or filled area are rendered using the fillStyle and strokeStyle properties. Both accept CSS-style color strings, as well as CanvasGradient and CanvasPattern objects that describe gradients and patterns. To create a gradient, use the createLinearGradient() or createRadialGradient() methods. To create a pattern, use createPattern().

To specify an opaque color using CSS notation, use a string of the form "#RRGGBB", where RR, GG, and BB are hexadecimal digits that specify the red, green, and blue components of the color as values between 00 and FF. For example, bright red is "#FF0000". To specify a partially transparent color, use a string of the form "rgba(R,G,B,A)". In this form, R, G, and B specify the red, green, and blue components of the color as decimal integers between 0 and 255, and A specifies the alpha (opacity) component as a floating-point value between 0.0 (fully transparent) and 1.0 (fully opaque). For example, half-transparent bright red is "rgba(255,0,0,0.5)".

See "Colors, Transparency, Gradients, and Patterns" on page 23 for more on these topics.

### Line width, line caps, and line joins

Canvas defines several properties that specify how lines are stroked. You can specify the width of the line with the lineWidth property, how the endpoints of lines are drawn with the lineCap property, and how lines are joined using the lineJoin property. See "Line-Drawing Attributes" on page 28 for examples of these graphics attributes.

### Drawing rectangles

You can outline and fill rectangles with strokeRect() and fillRect(). In addition, you can clear the area defined by a rectangle with clearRect(). See "Rectangles" on page 23.

### Drawing images

In the Canvas API, images are specified using Image objects that represent HTML <img> elements or offscreen images created with the Image() constructor. A <canvas> element or <video> element can also be used as an image source.

You can draw an image into a canvas with the `drawImage()` method, which, in its most general form, allows an arbitrary rectangular region of the source image to be scaled and rendered into the canvas. See "Images" on page 36.

### Drawing text

The `fillText()` method draws text and the `strokeText()` method draws outlined text. The `font` property specifies the font to use; the value of this property should be a CSS font specification string. The `textAlign` property specifies whether text is left-justified, centered, or right-justified on the X coordinate you pass, and the `textBaseline` property specifies where the text is drawn in relation to the Y coordinate you pass. See "Text" on page 30 for examples.

### Coordinate space and transformations

By default, the coordinate space for a canvas has its origin at (0,0) in the upper-left corner of the canvas, with *x* values increasing to the right and *y* values increasing down. The `width` and `height` attributes of the `<canvas>` tag specify the maximum X and Y coordinates, and a single unit in this coordinate space normally translates to a single onscreen pixel.

You can define your own coordinate space, and the coordinates you pass to the canvas drawing methods will automatically be transformed. This is done with the `translate()`, `scale()`, and `rotate()` methods, which affect the *transformation matrix* of the canvas. Because the coordinate space can be transformed like this, the coordinates you pass to methods such as `lineTo()` may not be measured in pixels and the Canvas API uses floating-point numbers instead of integers. Canvas coordinate space and transformations are explained in more detail in "Canvas Dimensions and Coordinates" on page 12 and "Coordinate System Transforms" on page 14.

### Shadows

The CRC can automatically add a drop shadow to anything you draw. The color of the shadow is specified with `shadowColor`, and its offset is changed using `shadowOffsetX` and `shadowOffsetY`. In addition, the amount of feathering applied to the shadow's edge may be set with `shadowBlur`. See "Shadows" on page 34 for examples.

## Compositing

Usually, when you draw on a canvas, the newly drawn graphics appear on top of the previous content of the canvas, partially or fully obscuring the old content, depending on the opacity of the new graphics. The process of combining new pixels with old pixels is called "compositing," and you can alter the way the canvas composites pixels by specifying different values for the globalCompositeOperation property. For example, you can set this property so that newly drawn graphics appear underneath the existing content. See CRC.globalCompositeOperation for a table of the possible options, and see "Compositing" on page 39 for figures that demonstrate the compositing operations.

## Saving graphics state

The save() and restore() methods allow you to save and restore the state of a CRC object. save() pushes the current state onto a stack, and restore() pops the most recently saved state off the top of the stack and sets the current drawing state based on those stored values.

All properties of the CRC object (except for the canvas property, which is a constant) are part of the saved state. The transformation matrix and clipping region are also part of the state, but the current path and current point are not. "Graphics Attributes" on page 10 has more on saving and restoring the graphics state.

## Manipulating pixels

The getImageData() method allows you to query the raw pixels of a canvas, and putImageData() allows you to set individual pixels. These can be useful if you want to implement image processing operations in JavaScript. See "Pixel Manipulation" on page 43 for an example.

---

# CRC.arc()                                 adds an arc, using a center point and radius

## Synopsis

```
void arc(float x, float y, float radius,
         float startAngle, endAngle,
         boolean counterclockwise)
```

---

CRC.arcTo()

## Arguments

*x, y*

> The coordinates of the center of the circle describing the arc.

*radius*

> The radius of the circle describing the arc.

*startAngle, endAngle*

> The angles that specify the start and endpoints of the arc along the circle. These angles are measured in radians. The three o'clock position along the positive X axis is an angle of 0, and angles increase in the clockwise direction.

*counterclockwise*

> Whether the arc is traversed counterclockwise (true) or clockwise (false) along the circle's circumference.

## Description

The first five arguments to this method specify a start point and an endpoint on the circumference of a circle. Invoking this method adds a straight line between the current point and the start point to the current subpath. Next it adds the arc along the circumference of the circle between the start and endpoints to the subpath. The final argument specifies the direction in which the circle should be traversed to connect the start and endpoints. This method leaves the current point set to the endpoint of the arc.

## See Also

CRC.arcTo(), CRC.beginPath(), CRC.closePath()

---

## CRC.arcTo()                 adds an arc, using two tangent lines and a radius

### Synopsis

```
void arcTo(float x1, float y1,
           float x2, float y2,
           float radius)
```

### Arguments

*x1, y1*

> The coordinates of point P1

---

*x2, y2*

The coordinates of point P2

*radius*

The radius of the circle that defines the arc

### Description

This method adds a straight line and an arc to the current subpath and describes that arc in a way that makes it particularly useful for adding rounded corners to polygons. The arc that is added to the path is a portion of a circle with the specified *radius*. The arc has one point that is tangent to the line from the current position to P1 and one point that is tangent to the line from P1 to P2. The arc begins and ends at these two tangent points and is drawn in the direction that connects those two points with the shortest arc. Before adding the arc to the path, this method adds a straight line from the current point to the start point of the arc. After calling this method, the current point is at the endpoint of the arc, which lies on the line between P1 and P2.

### Example

Given a context object c, you can draw a 100 × 100 square with rounded corners (of varying radii) with code like this:

```
c.beginPath();
c.moveTo(150, 100);              // Start at the top middle
c.arcTo(200,100,200,200,40);     // Top edge and upper right
c.arcTo(200,200,100,200,30);     // Right edge and lower right
c.arcTo(100,200,100,100,20);     // Bottom and lower left
c.arcTo(100,100,200,100,10);     // Left and upper left
c.closePath();                    // Back to the starting point
c.stroke();                       // Draw the path
```

### See Also

CRC.arc()

---

## CRC.beginPath()                     starts a new path in a canvas

### Synopsis

```
void beginPath()
```

---

CRC.bezierCurveTo()

## Description

beginPath() discards any currently defined path and begins a new one. There is no current point after a call to beginPath().

When the context for a canvas is first created, beginPath() is implicitly called.

## See Also

CRC.closePath(), CRC.fill(), CRC.stroke()

---

# CRC.bezierCurveTo()       adds a cubic Bézier curve to the current subpath

## Synopsis

```
void bezierCurveTo(float cpX1, float cpY1,
                   float cpX2, float cpY2,
                   float x, float y)
```

## Arguments

cpX1, cpY1

> The coordinates of the control point associated with the curve's start point (the current position)

cpX2, cpY2

> The coordinates of the control point associated with the curve's endpoint

x, y

> The coordinates of the curve's endpoint

## Description

bezierCurveTo() adds a cubic Bézier curve to the current subpath of a canvas. The start point of the curve is the current point of the canvas, and the endpoint is (x,y). The two Bézier control points (cpX1, cpY1) and (cpX2, cpY2) define the shape of the curve. When this method returns, the current position is (x,y).

## See Also

CRC.quadraticCurveTo()

---

## CRC.clearRect()                    *erases a rectangular area of a canvas*

### Synopsis

```
void clearRect(float x, float y,
               float width, float height)
```

### Arguments

*x, y*

    The coordinates of the upper-left corner of the rectangle

*width, height*

    The dimensions of the rectangle

### Description

clearRect() fills the specified rectangle with transparent black. Unlike rect(), it does not affect the current point or the current path.

## CRC.clip()                          *sets the clipping region of a canvas*

### Synopsis

```
void clip()
```

### Description

This method computes the intersection of the inside of the current path with the current clipping region and uses that (smaller) region as the new clipping region. Note that there is no way to enlarge the clipping region. If you want a temporary clipping region, you should first call save() so that you can later restore() the original clipping region. The default clipping region for a canvas is the canvas rectangle itself.

Like the fill() method, clip() treats all subpaths as closed and uses the nonzero winding rule for distinguishing the inside of the path from the outside of the path.

## CRC.closePath()                    closes an open subpath

### Synopsis

```
void closePath()
```

### Description

If the current subpath of the canvas is open, closePath() closes it by adding a line connecting the current point to the first point of the subpath. It then begins a new subpath (as if by calling moveTo()) at that same point.

fill() and clip() treat all subpaths as if they had been closed, so you only need to call closePath() explicitly if you want to stroke() a closed path.

### See Also

CRC.beginPath(), CRC.fill(), CRC.moveTo(), CRC.stroke()

## CRC.createImageData()            creates a new ImageData object

### Synopsis

```
ImageData createImageData(w, h)
ImageData createImageData(ImageData data)
```

### Arguments

*w, h*

The desired ImageData width and height, in CSS pixels

data

An existing ImageData object that specifies the size of the ImageData to be created

### Returns

A newly created ImageData object that has the specified width and height or has the same size as *data*.

### Description

Returns a new ImageData object with the specified width and height or the same dimensions as *data*. All pixels within this new

ImageData object are initialized to transparent black (all color components and alpha are 0).

The *w* and *h* arguments specify image dimensions in CSS pixels. Implementations are allowed to map single CSS pixels to more than one underlying device pixel. The `width` and `height` properties of the returned ImageData object specify the image dimensions in device pixels, and these values may not match the *w* and *h* arguments.

### See Also

CRC.getImageData(), CRC.putImageData()

---

## CRC.createLinearGradient()                    create a linear color gradient

### Synopsis

```
CanvasGradient createLinearGradient(float xStart,
                                    float yStart,
                                    float xEnd,
                                    float yEnd)
```

### Arguments

*xStart, yStart*
>   The coordinates of the gradient's start point

*xEnd, yEnd*
>   The coordinates of the gradient's endpoint

### Returns

A CanvasGradient object representing a linear color gradient.

### Description

This method creates and returns a new CanvasGradient object that linearly interpolates colors between the specified start point and endpoint. Note that this method does not specify any colors for the gradient. Use the `addColorStop()` method of the returned object to do that. To stroke lines or fill areas using a gradient, assign a CanvasGradient object to the `strokeStyle` or `fillStyle` properties.

### See Also

CanvasGradient.addColorStop(), CRC.createRadialGradient()

---

## CRC.createPattern()                    creates a pattern of tiled images

### Synopsis

```
CanvasPattern createPattern(image,
                            String repetitionStyle)
```

### Arguments

*image*
> The image to be tiled, specified as an <img>, <canvas>, or
> <video> tag, or as an offscreen image created with the
> Image() constructor.

*repetitionStyle*
> Specifies how the image is tiled. The possible values are in the
> following table:

| Value | Meaning |
|---|---|
| "repeat" | Tile the image in both directions. This is the default. |
| "repeat-x" | Tile the image in the X dimension only. |
| "repeat-y" | Tile the image in the Y dimension only. |
| "no-repeat" | Do not tile the image; use it only a single time. |

### Returns

A CanvasPattern object representing the pattern.

### Description

This method creates and returns a CanvasPattern object that represents the pattern defined by a tiled image. To use a pattern for stroking lines or filling areas, use a CanvasPattern object as the value of the strokeStyle or fillStyle properties.

### See Also

CanvasPattern

# CRC.createRadialGradient()

## Synopsis

```
CanvasGradient createRadialGradient(float xStart,
                                    float yStart,
                                    float radiusStart,
                                    float xEnd,
                                    float yEnd,
                                    float radiusEnd)
```

## Arguments

*xStart, yStart*
> The coordinates of the center of the starting circle

*radiusStart*
> The radius of the starting circle

*xEnd, yEnd*
> The coordinates of the center of the ending circle

*radiusEnd*
> The radius of the ending circle

## Returns

A CanvasGradient object representing a radial color gradient.

## Description

This method creates and returns a new CanvasGradient object that radially interpolates colors between the circumferences of the two specified circles. Note that this method does not specify any colors for the gradient. Use the addColorStop() method of the returned object to do that. To stroke lines or fill areas using a gradient, assign a CanvasGradient object to the strokeStyle or fillStyle properties.

Radial gradients are rendered by using the color at offset 0 for the circumference of the first circle, the color at offset 1 for the second circle, and interpolated color values at circles between the two.

## See Also

CanvasGradient.addColorStop(), CRC.createLinearGradient()

# CRC.drawImage()                                          draws an image

## Synopsis

```
void drawImage(image, float dx, float dy)
void drawImage(image, float dx, float dy,
               float dw, float dh)
void drawImage(image, float sx, float sy,
               float sw, float sh,
               float dx, float dy,
               float dw, float dh)
```

## Arguments

*image*

> The image to be drawn. This should be a document element
> representing an <img>, <canvas>, or <video> tag. You can also
> use offscreen images created with the Image() constructor.

*dx, dy*

> The point on the destination canvas at which the upper-left
> corner of the image is drawn.

*dw, dh*

> The width and height at which the image should be drawn
> onto the destination canvas. If these arguments are omitted,
> the image will be copied at its natural size.

*sx, sy*

> The upper-left corner of the region of the source image that is
> to be drawn. These arguments are measured in image pixels.
> Specify these arguments if you want to copy only a portion of
> the source image.

*sw, sh*

> The width and height, in image pixels, of the region of the
> source image that is to be drawn onto the canvas.

## Description

There are three variants of this method. The first copies the entire
image to the canvas, placing its upper-left corner at the specified
point and mapping each image pixel to one unit in the canvas coordinate system. The second variant also copies the entire image to
the canvas but allows you to specify the desired width and height
of the image in canvas units. The third variant is fully general: it

allows you to specify any rectangular region of the image and copy it, with arbitrary scaling to any position within the canvas. Note that *dx*, *dy*, *dw*, and *dh* are transformed by the current transformation matrix, but that *sx*, *sy*, *sw*, and *sh* are not transformed.

drawImage() expects its image data to be ready for immediate use, which is why it does not allow you to specify the URL of an image to display. If you specify an <img> or <video> tag that is still loading its associated image or video, the call to drawImage() will return immediately without drawing anything.

## CRC.fill()                                                   fills the path

### Synopsis

```
void fill()
```

### Description

fill() fills the current path with the color, gradient, or pattern specified by the fillStyle property. Any subpaths that are not closed are filled as if the closePath() method had been called on them. (Note, however, that this does not actually cause those subpaths to become closed.)

Filling a path does not clear the path. You may call stroke() after calling fill() without redefining the path.

When the path intersects itself or when subpaths overlap, fill() uses the "nonzero winding rule" to determine which points are inside the path and which are outside. This means, for example, that if your path defines a square inside of a circle and the square's subpath winds in the opposite direction of the circle's path, then the interior of the square will be outside of the path and will not be filled.

### See Also

CRC.fillRect()

## CRC.fillRect()

fills a rectangle

### Synopsis

```
void fillRect(float x, float y,
              float width, float height)
```

### Arguments

*x, y*

The coordinates of the upper-left corner of the rectangle

*width, height*

The dimensions of the rectangle

### Description

fillRect() fills the specified rectangle with the color, gradient, or pattern specified by the fillStyle property.

Unlike the rect() method, fillRect() has no effect on the current point or the current path.

### See Also

CRC.fill(), CRC.rect(), CRC.strokeRect()

---

## CRC.fillText()

draws text

### Synopsis

```
void fillText(String text, float x, float y,float max)
```

### Arguments

*text*

The text to draw in the canvas.

*x, y*

The "anchor point" of the text in the canvas. The interpretation of this point depends on the values of the textAlign and textBaseline properties.

*max*

This optional argument specifies a maximum width for the text. If the *text* would be wider than *max* when drawn using the font property and the current transformation, then the text

---

will be drawn using a smaller or more condensed version of the font instead.

### Description

fillText() draws *text* using the current font and fillStyle properties. The *x* and *y* arguments specify where on the canvas the text should be drawn, but the interpretation of these arguments depends on the textAlign and textBaseline properties, respectively.

If textAlign is "left" or is "start" (the default) for a canvas that uses left-to-right text (also the default) or "end" for a canvas that uses right-to-left text, then the text is drawn to the right of the specified X coordinate. If textAlign is "center", then the text is horizontally centered around the specified X coordinate. Otherwise (if textAlign is "right", is "end" for left-to-right text, or is "start" for right-to-left text) the text is drawn to the left of the specified X coordinate.

If textBaseline is "alphabetic" (the default), "bottom", or "ideographic", most of the glyphs will appear above the specified Y coordinate. If textBaseline is "center", the text will be approximately vertically centered on the specified Y coordinate. And if textBaseline is "top" or "hanging", most of the glyphs will appear below the specified Y coordinate.

### See Also

CRC.strokeText()

---

## CRC.getImageData()                    gets individual pixels from a canvas

### Synopsis

    ImageData getImageData(x, y, w, h)

### Arguments

*x, y*

> The coordinates of one corner (usually the upper-left) of the rectangular region of pixels to be returned. These arguments are not transformed by the current transformation matrix.

*w, h*

> The width and height of the rectangle of pixels to be returned. These arguments are not transformed by the current

---

transformation matrix. These arguments are usually positive, but negative values are allowed.

### Returns

A newly-created ImageData object that contains the pixel values for all pixels within the rectangle.

### Description

The arguments to this method are untransformed coordinates that specify a rectangular region of the canvas. The method copies the pixel data from that region of the canvas into a new ImageData object and returns that object. See ImageData for an explanation of how to access the red, green, blue, and alpha components of the individual pixels.

The RGB color components of the returned pixels are not premultiplied by the alpha value. If any portions of the requested rectangle lie outside the bounds of the canvas, the associated pixels in the ImageData are set to transparent black (all zeros). If the implementation uses more than one device pixel per CSS pixel then the width and height properties of the returned ImageData object will be different than the w and h arguments.

Like Canvas.toDataURL(), this method is subject to a security check to prevent cross-origin information leakage. getImageData() only returns an ImageData object if the underlying canvas is "origin-clean"; otherwise, it raises an exception. A canvas is not origin-clean if it has ever had an image drawn in it (directly by drawImage() or indirectly through a CanvasPattern) that has a different origin than the document that contains the canvas.

### See Also

CRC.putImageData(), ImageData

---

## CRC.globalCompositeOperation   how colors are combined on the canvas

### Synopsis

```
String globalCompositeOperation
```

---

## Description

This property specifies how source pixels being rendered onto the canvas are combined (or "composited") with the destination pixels that already exist in the canvas. This property is typically useful only when you are working with partially transparent colors or have set the globalAlpha property. The default is value is "source-over". Other commonly used values are "destination-over" and "copy".

The following table lists the allowed property values and their meanings. In the third column, the word *source* refers to the pixels being drawn onto the canvas, the word *destination* refers to the existing pixels on the canvas, and the word *result* refers to the pixels that result from the combination of the source and destination. The second column shows the formula for computing a result pixel from a source pixel S and a destination pixel D along with the alpha channel (the opacity) of the source pixel $\alpha_s$ and the alpha channel of the destination $\alpha_d$:

| Value | Formula | Meaning |
|---|---|---|
| copy | S | Draw the source pixel, ignoring the destination pixel. |
| destination-atop | $(1-\alpha_d)S + \alpha_s D$ | Draw the source pixel underneath the destination. If the source is transparent, the result is also transparent. |
| destination-in | $\alpha_s D$ | Multiply the destination pixel by the opacity of the source pixel, but ignore the color of the source. |
| destination-out | $(1-\alpha_s)D$ | The destination pixel is made transparent when the source is opaque and is left unchanged when the source is transparent. The color of the source pixel is ignored. |
| destination-over | $(1-\alpha_d)S + D$ | The source pixel appears behind the destination pixel, showing through based on the transparency of the destination. |
| lighter | S + D | The color components of the two pixels are simply added together and clipped if the sum exceeds the maximum value. |

| Value | Formula | Meaning |
|-------|---------|---------|
| source-atop | $\alpha_d S + (1-\alpha_s)D$ | Draw the source pixel on top of the destination but multiply it by the opacity of the destination. Don't draw anything over a transparent destination. |
| source-in | $\alpha_d S$ | Draw the source pixel, but multiply it by the opacity of the destination. The color of the destination is ignored. If the destination is transparent, the result is transparent, too. |
| source-out | $(1-\alpha_d)S$ | The result is the source pixel where the destination is transparent, and transparent pixels where the destination is opaque. The color of the destination is ignored. |
| source-over | $S + (1-\alpha_s)D$ | The source pixel is drawn on top of the destination pixel. If the source is translucent, then the destination pixel contributes to the result. This is the default value of the global CompositeOperation property. |
| xor | $(1-\alpha d)S + (1-\alpha s)D$ | If the source is transparent, the result is the destination. If the destination is transparent, the result is the source. If source and destination are both transparent or both opaque, then the result is transparent. |

## CRC.isPointInPath()

**tests whether a path encloses a point**

### Synopsis

```
boolean isPointInPath(float x, float y)
```

### Arguments

*x,y*

> The point to be tested. Note that these are in raw canvas coordinates, and are not transformed by the current transformation matrix.

## Returns

true if the specified point falls within or on the edge of the current path, and false otherwise.

## Description

isPointInPath() tests whether the specified point is inside (or on the boundary of) the current path. The specified point is not transformed by the current transformation matrix. *x* should be a value between 0 and canvas.width and *y* should be a value between 0 and canvas.height.

## Example

The reason that isPointInPath() tests untransformed points is that it is designed for "hit testing": determining whether a user's mouse click (for example) is on top of the portion of the canvas described by the path. In order to do hit testing, mouse coordinates must first be translated so that they are relative to the canvas rather than the window. If the canvas's size on the screen is different than the size declared by its width and height attributes (if style.width and style.height have been set, for example) then the mouse coordinates also have to be scaled to match the canvas coordinates. The following function is designed for use as an onclick handler of a <canvas> and performs the necessary transformation to convert mouse coordinates to canvas coordinates:

```
// An onclick handler for a canvas tag.
// Assumes a path is currently defined.
function hittest(ev) {
    // Get context, assuming this is the canvas
    var c = this.getContext("2d");

    // Get the canvas size and position
    var bb = this.getBoundingClientRect();

    // Convert mouse event coordinates to canvas coords
    var x = (ev.clientX-bb.left)*(this.width/bb.width);
    var y = (ev.clientY-bb.top)*(this.height/bb.height);

    // Fill the path if the user clicked on it
    if (c.isPointInPath(x,y)) c.fill();
}
```

## CRC.lineCap                              specifies how the ends of lines are rendered

### Synopsis

```
String lineCap
```

### Description

The lineCap property specifies how lines should be terminated. It matters only when drawing wide lines. Legal values for this property are listed in the following table. The default value is "butt":

| Value | Meaning |
| --- | --- |
| "butt" | This default value specifies that the line should have no cap. The end of the line is straight and is perpendicular to the direction of the line. The line is not extended beyond its endpoint. |
| "round" | This value specifies that lines should be capped with a semicircle whose diameter is equal to the width of the line and that extends beyond the end of the line by one half the width of the line. |
| "square" | This value specifies that lines should be capped with a rectangle. This value is like "butt", but the line is extended by half of its width. |

### See Also

CRC.lineJoin

## CRC.lineJoin                              specifies how vertices are rendered

### Synopsis

```
String lineJoin
```

### Description

When a path includes vertices where line segments and/or curves meet, the lineJoin property specifies how those vertices are drawn. The effect of this property is apparent only when drawing with wide lines.

The default value of the property is "miter", which specifies that the outside edges of the two line segments are extended until they intersect. When two lines meet at an acute angle, mitered joins can become quite long. The miterLimit property places an upper bound on the length of a miter. If a miter would exceed this limit, it is converted to a bevel.

The value "round" specifies that the outside edges of the vertex should be joined with a filled arc whose diameter is equal to the width of the line.

The value "bevel" specifies that the outside edges of the vertex should be joined with a filled triangle.

### See Also

CRC.lineCap, CRC.miterLimit

## CRC.lineTo()                    adds a straight line to the current subpath

### Synopsis

```
void lineTo(float x, float y)
```

### Arguments

*x, y*
> The coordinates of the endpoint of the line

### Description

lineTo() adds a straight line to the current subpath. The line begins at the current point and ends at (x,y). When this method returns, the current position is (x,y).

### See Also

CRC.beginPath(), CRC.moveTo()

## CRC.measureText()              computes the width of the specified text

### Synopsis

```
TextMetrics measureText(String text)
```

### Arguments

*text*
> The string of text to be measured

### Returns

A TextMetrics object whose width property specifies the width that *text* would occupy if it were drawn with the current font.

### Description

measureText() measures the specified text and returns a TextMetrics object containing the results of the measurement. At the time of this writing, the returned object has only a single width property, and the text height and bounding box are not measured.

### See Also

TextMetrics

---

# CRC.miterLimit                    maximum miter length to line width ratio

### Synopsis

```
float miterLimit
```

### Description

When lines are drawn with the lineJoin property set to "miter" and two lines meet at an acute angle, the resulting miter can be quite long. When miters are too long, they become visually jarring. This miterLimit property places an upper bound on the length of the miter. This property expresses a ratio of the miter length to half the line width. The default value is 10, which means that a miter should never be longer than five times the line width. If a miter formed by two lines would be longer than the maximum allowed by miterLimit then those two lines will be joined with a bevel instead of a miter.

### See Also

CRC.lineJoin

---

# CRC.moveTo()    sets the current position and begins a new subpath

## Synopsis

```
void moveTo(float x, float y)
```

## Arguments

*x, y*

> The coordinates of the new current point

## Description

moveTo() sets the current position to (x,y) and begins a new subpath with this as its first point. If there was a previous subpath and it consisted of just one point, that empty subpath is removed from the path.

## See Also

CRC.beginPath()

---

# CRC.putImageData()    copies pixels from an ImageData into the canvas

## Synopsis

```
void putImageData(ImageData data, float dx, float dy,
                  float sx, float sy, float sw, float sh)
```

## Arguments

*data*

> An ImageData object.

*dx, dy*

> The coordinates of a *destination* point in the canvas. Pixels from *data* will be copied to the canvas starting at this point. These arguments are not transformed by the current transformation matrix.

*sx, sy, sw, sh*

> These optional arguments specify a source rectangle within the ImageData. If specified, only the pixels within that rectangle will be copied to the canvas. If omitted, all pixels in the ImageData will be copied. If these arguments specify a rectangle that exceeds the bounds of the ImageData, the rectangle will

be clipped to those bounds. Negative values for *sx* and *sy* are allowed.

## Description

putImageData() copies a rectangular block of pixels from an Image-Data object onto the canvas. This is a low-level pixel copy operation: the globalCompositeOperation and globalAlpha attributes are ignored as are the clipping region, transformation matrix, and shadow-drawing attributes.

One use for ImageData objects is as a "backing store" for a canvas—saving a copy of the canvas pixels in an ImageData object (using getImageData()) allows you to draw temporarily on the canvas and then restore it to its original state with putImageData().

## See Also

CRC.createImageData(), CRC.getImageData(), ImageData

---

## CRC.quadraticCurveTo()        adds a quadratic Bézier curve to the path

### Synopsis

```
void quadraticCurveTo(float cpX, float cpY,
                      float x, float y)
```

### Arguments

*cpX, cpY*
    The coordinates of the control point

*x, y*
    The coordinates of the endpoint of the curve

### Description

This method adds a quadratic Bézier curve segment to the current subpath. The curve starts at the current point and ends at (x,y). The control point (cpX, cpY) specifies the shape of the curve between these two points. (The mathematics of Bézier curves is beyond the scope of this book, however.) When this method returns, the current position is (x,y).

---

### See Also

CRC.bezierCurveTo()

---

## CRC.rect() adds a rectangle subpath to the path

### Synopsis

```
void rect(float x, float y,
          float width, float height)
```

### Arguments

*x, y*
> The coordinates of the upper-left corner of the rectangle

*width, height*
> The dimensions of the rectangle

### Description

This method adds a rectangle to the path. This rectangle is in a subpath of its own and is not connected to any other subpaths in the path. When this method returns, the current position is $(x,y)$. A call to this method is equivalent to the following sequence of calls:

```
c.moveTo(x,y);
c.lineTo(x+w, y);
c.lineTo(x+w, y+h);
c.lineTo(x, y+h);
c.closePath();
```

### See Also

CRC.fillRect(), CRC.strokeRect()

---

## CRC.restore() resets drawing state to saved values

### Synopsis

```
void restore()
```

---

CRC.rotate()

### Description

This method pops the stack of saved graphics states and restores the values of the CRC properties, the clipping path, and the transformation matrix. See the save() method for further information.

### See Also

CRC.save()

---

## CRC.rotate()                                    adds a rotation to current transform

### Synopsis

```
void rotate(float angle)
```

### Arguments

*angle*

> The rotation, in radians. Positive values result in clockwise rotation, and negative values result in counterclockwise rotation.

### Description

This method alters the current transformation matrix so that any subsequent drawing appears rotated within the canvas by the specified angle. It does not rotate the <canvas> element itself. Note that the angle is specified in radians. To convert degrees to radians, multiply by Math.PI and divide by 180.

### See Also

CRC.scale(), CRC.translate()

---

## CRC.save()                                    saves a copy of the current graphics state

### Synopsis

```
void save()
```

### Description

save() pushes a copy of the current graphics state onto a stack of saved graphics states. This allows you to temporarily change the

---

graphics state, and then restore the previous values with a call to
restore().

The graphics state of a canvas includes all the properties of the CRC
object (except for the read-only canvas property). It also includes
the transformation matrix that is the result of calls to rotate(),
scale(), and translate(). Additionally, it includes the clipping
path, which is specified with the clip() method. Note, however,
that the current path and current position are not part of the graphics state and are not saved by this method.

### See Also

CRC.restore()

---

## CRC.scale()                    adds a scaling operation to the current transform

### Synopsis

    void scale(float sx, float sy)

### Arguments

sx, sy
    The horizontal and vertical scaling factors

### Description

scale() adds a scale transformation to the current transformation
matrix of the canvas. Scaling is done with independent horizontal
and vertical scaling factors. For example, passing the values 2.0 and
0.5 causes subsequently drawn paths to be twice as wide and half
as high as they would otherwise have been. Specifying a negative
value for sx causes X coordinates to be flipped across the Y axis,
and a negative value of sy causes Y coordinates to be flipped across
the X axis.

### See Also

CRC.rotate(), CRC.translate()

# CRC.setTransform()

### Synopsis

```
void setTransform(float a, float b,
                  float c, float d,
                  float e, float f)
```

### Arguments

*a, b, c, d, e, f*
    Six elements of a 3 × 3 affine transformation matrix

### Description

This method allows you to set the current transformation matrix directly rather than through a series of calls to translate(), scale(), and rotate(). After calling this method, the new transformation is:

```
x'   a c e   x   = ax + cy + e
y' = b d f × y   = bx + dy + f
1    0 0 1   1
```

### Example

You can temporarily reset the transformation of a context c to the identity transform, so that you can work with raw canvas coordinates, using code like this:

```
c.save();                    // Save current transform
c.setTransform(1,0,0,1,0,0); // Set identity transform
/* Now use raw canvas coordinates here */
c.restore();                 // Revert to old transform
```

### See Also

CRC.rotate(), CRC.scale(), CRC.transform(), CRC.translate()

---

# CRC.stroke()

### Synopsis

```
void stroke()
```

---

## Description

The stroke() method draws the outline of the current path. The path defines the geometry of the line that is produced, but the visual appearance of that line depends on the strokeStyle, lineWidth, lineCap, lineJoin, and miterLimit properties.

The term *stroke* refers to a pen or brush stroke. It means "draw the outline of." Contrast this stroke() method with fill(), which fills the interior of a path rather than stroking the outline of the path.

## See Also

CRC.fill(), CRC.lineCap, CRC.lineJoin, CRC.strokeRect()

# CRC.strokeRect()                                     draws a rectangle

## Synopsis

```
void strokeRect(float x, float y,
                float width, float height)
```

## Arguments

*x, y*
>    The coordinates of the upper-left corner of the rectangle

*width, height*
>    The dimensions of the rectangle

## Description

This method draws the outline (but does not fill the interior) of a rectangle with the specified position and size. Line color and line width are specified by the strokeStyle and lineWidth properties. The appearance of the rectangle corners are specified by the line Join property.

Unlike the rect() method, strokeRect() has no effect on the current path or the current point.

## See Also

CRC.fillRect(), CRC.lineJoin, CRC.rect(), CRC.stroke()

## CRC.strokeText()                          draws outlined text

### Synopsis

```
void strokeText(String text, float x, float y,float max)
```

### Arguments

*text*
> The text to draw in the canvas

*x, y*
> The "anchor point" of the text in the canvas

*max*
> An optional maximum width for the text

### Description

strokeText() works just like fillText() except that instead of filling the individual character glyphs with fillStyle, it strokes the outline of each glyph using strokeStyle. strokeText() produces interesting graphical effects when used at large font sizes, but fillText() is more commonly used for actually drawing text.

### See Also

CRC.fillText()

---

## CRC.transform()                          performs an arbitrary transform

### Synopsis

```
void transform(float a, float b,
               float c, float d,
               float e, float f)
```

### Arguments

*a, b, c, d, e, f*
> Six elements of a $3 \times 3$ affine transformation matrix

### Description

The arguments to this method specify the six nontrivial elements of a $3 \times 3$ affine transformation matrix T:

---

```
a c e
b d f
0 0 1
```

`transform()` sets the current transformation matrix to the product of the transformation matrix and the T:

```
CTM' = CTM × T
```

Translations, scales, and rotations can be implemented in terms of this general-purpose `transform()` method. For a translation, call `transform(1,0,0,1,dx,dy)`. For a scale, call `transform(sx,0,0,sy, 0,0)`. For a clockwise rotation around the origin by an angle x, use:

```
transform(cos(x),sin(x),-sin(x), cos(x), 0, 0)
```

For a shear by a factor of k parallel to the X axis, call `transform(1,0,k,1,0,0)`. For a shear parallel to the Y axis, call `transform(1,k,0,1,0,0)`.

## Example

```
// Perform a shear transform
function shear(c,kx,ky) { c.transform(1,ky,kx,1,0,0); }

// Rotate clockwise by theta radians about the point (x,y)
function rotateAbout(c, theta, x, y) {
    var ct = Math.cos(theta);
    var st = Math.sin(theta);
    c.transform(ct, -st, st, ct,
                -x*ct - y*st + x,
                x*st - y*ct + y);
}
```

## See Also

CRC.rotate(), CRC.scale(), CRC.setTransform(), CRC.translate()

---

## CRC.translate()                    adds a translation to the current transform

### Synopsis

```
void translate(float dx, float dy)
```

### Arguments

*dx, dy*

　　The amounts to translate in the X and Y dimensions

---

ImageData

## Description

`translate()` adds horizontal and vertical offsets to the transformation matrix of the canvas. The arguments *dx* and *dy* are added to all points in any subsequently defined paths.

## See Also

`CRC.rotate()`, `CRC.scale()`

---

**ImageData**                         an array of pixel data for an image

## Properties

`data`
> A read-only reference to an array-like object that contains the image data

`height`
> The number of rows of image data

`width`
> The number of pixels per row of data

## Description

An ImageData object holds the red, green, blue, and alpha components of a rectangular region of pixels. Obtain an ImageData object with the `createImageData()` or `getImageData()` methods of the CanvasRenderingContext2D object of a `<canvas>` tag.

The `width` and `height` properties specify the dimensions of the rectangle of pixels. The `data` property is an array that holds the pixel data. Pixels appear in the `data[]` array in left-to-right and top-to-bottom order. Each pixel consists of four byte values that represent the R, G, B, and A components, in that order. Thus, the color components for a pixel at (x,y) within an ImageData object `image` can be accessed like this:

```
var offset = (x + y*image.width) * 4;
var red = image.data[offset];
var green = image.data[offset+1];
var blue = image.data[offset+2];
var alpha = image.data[offset+3];
```

---

The data[] array is not a true JavaScript array, but an array-like object known as a CanvasPixelArray object. (CanvasPixelArray is documented here, and does not have its own entry in this reference section.) A CanvasPixelArray is an optimized array of bytes. The elements of this array must be integers between 0 and 255. The elements are read/write, but the length of the array is fixed. For any ImageData object i, i.data.length will always equal i.width * i.height * 4.

## See Also

CRC, CRC.getImageData()

---

## TextMetrics
measurements of a string of text

### Properties

width
    The width of the specified text

### Description

A TextMetrics object is returned by the measureText() method of CanvasRenderingContext2D. Its width property holds the width of the measured text, in CSS pixels.

### See Also

CRC.measureText()

# Index

We'd like to hear your suggestions for improving our indexes. Send email to
*index@oreilly.com*.

# Related Titles from O'Reilly

## Web Authoring & Design

ActionScript 3.0 Cookbook

Ajax Hacks

Ambient Findability

Creating a Web Site: The Missing Manual, *2nd Edition*

CSS Cookbook, *2nd Edition*

CSS Pocket Reference, *3rd Edition*

CSS: The Definitive Guide, *3rd Edition*

CSS: The Missing Manual, *2nd Edition*

Dreamweaver 8 Design and Construction

Dreamweaver 8: The Missing Manual

Dreamweaver CS4: The Missing Manual

Dynamic HTML: The Definitive Reference, *3rd Edition*

Essential ActionScript 3.0

Facebook: The Missing Manual

FBML Essentials

Flex 3 Cookbook

Flash 8: Projects for Learning Animation and Interactivity

Flash 8: The Missing Manual

Flash Hacks

Getting Started with Flex 3

Head First Ajax

Head First HTML with CSS & XHTML

Head First Web Design

High Performance Web Sites

HTML & XHTML: The Definitive Guide, *6th Edition*

HTML & XHTML Pocket Reference, *3rd Edition*

Information Architecture for the World Wide Web, *3rd Edition*

Information Dashboard Design

JavaScript: The Definitive Guide, *5th Edition*

JavaScript & DHTML Cookbook, *2nd Edition*

Learning ActionScript 3.0

Learning Flex 3

Learning JavaScript, *2nd Edition*

Learning Web Design, *3rd Edition*

Painting the Web

PHP Hacks

Programming Collective Intelligence

Programming Flex 3

Search Engine Optimization for Flash

Web Design in a Nutshell, *3rd Edition*

Web Site Measurement Hacks

# O'REILLY®

# Get even more for your money.

**Join the O'Reilly Community, and register the O'Reilly books you own. It's free, and you'll get:**

- $4.99 ebook upgrade offer
- 40% upgrade offer on O'Reilly print books
- Membership discounts on books and events
- Free lifetime updates to ebooks and videos
- Multiple ebook formats, DRM FREE
- Participation in the O'Reilly community
- Newsletters
- Account management
- 100% Satisfaction Guarantee

**Registering your books is easy:**

1. Go to: oreilly.com/go/register
2. Create an O'Reilly login.
3. Provide your address.
4. Register your books.

Note: English-language books only

**To order books online:**
oreilly.com/store

**For questions about products or an order:**
orders@oreilly.com

**To sign up to get topic-specific email announcements and/or news about upcoming books, conferences, special offers, and new technologies:**
elists@oreilly.com

**For technical questions about book content:**
booktech@oreilly.com

**To submit new book proposals to our editors:**
proposals@oreilly.com

**O'Reilly books are available in multiple DRM-free ebook formats. For more information:**
oreilly.com/ebooks

# O'REILLY®

Spreading the knowledge of innovators     oreilly.com